USING LAW BOOKS

USING LAW BOOKS

Alfred J. Lewis
University of California—Davis

KENDALL/HUNT PUBLISHING COMPANY
Dubuque, Iowa

Library of Congress Catalog Card Number: 75-35385

ISBN 0—8403—1332—2

Printed in the United States of America

Contents

Preface

Using Law Books is designed as a beginner's manual in legal research. It should be a suitable text for paralegals, policemen, librarians and others, as well as beginning law students. They all bring the same state of ignorance to class and it is a mistake to treat them differently.

There are at least a half dozen general law texts in print. It was my experience, however, after teaching the subject to law students for several years to discover that none of the available texts were suitable. I was compelled to write my own, which has now become the genesis for this manual. The other texts, to a greater or lesser extent, tend to contain bibliographic descriptions of law books. They seldom discuss these books within the practical context of doing legal research. Of course, there is a need for one definitive *reference* on the bibliography of law. Price and Bitner's *Effective Legal Research* meets that need to the extent it is not outdated.

This manual attempts to reflect ten years of my own experience as a law librarian and teacher helping lawyers, law students, students and faculty from other disciplines, policemen, legal secretaries, and the general public find their way through a maze of legal literature. The descriptions of each type of law book have been restricted to essential details only. It is a common mistake to overwhelm beginners with too much information. Some details are immediately apparent when the book is used; others are matters of sophistication and simply cannot be learned at the beginning.

The style and organization of the writing is such that an initial, straight-through reading of a chapter should provide some general orientation. It is strongly urged, however, that subsequent readings be done in a law library with the appropriate set of books in front of the student. Writing this book is like writing a handbook on how to drive a car for those who do not have a car. There is not much a teacher or student can do if they do not get their hands on the subject matter. Other books on this topic generally provide pictures from the pages of other law books. I do not feel that this is helpful, however, because seeing the information on a sample page is only a small part of the entire context (which is, for example: seeing a certain page, in a certain supplement, to a certain labelled volume, that is part of a certain fifty volume set of books, that is situated in a certain collection, of a certain law library). Additionally, I believe the insertion of pictures at various points detracts from the manual's effectiveness as a readable, general guide . It is not ignorance of details that troubles the student so much as a more serious failure to see the overall pattern of legal publication.

Occasionally my prejudices regarding the relative usefulness of certain sets of law books have been set forth. I have found that it is difficult to offer guidance based on experience without indicating preferences.

The order of the chapters is another departure from other law texts which start out with case law first. This reflects the unique importance of court-made law in our Anglo-American common law heritage. It is also true that beginning courses in law school deal almost entirely with case law principles and are taught by the "case method." However, for the reasons set forth at the beginning of the chapter on statutory law, as a general rule one's research should start with the statutes first. Since the manual starts with statutes first, it was logical to continue on with matters of statutory interpretation (especially legislative history) and subsidiary legislation (local ordinances and administrative regulations).

California and federal materials have been emphasized and used as examples throughout. Notes on other state materials have been made. In any case, the pattern is the same for all jurisdictions. Legal publishing in the United States has been dominated by a very few large publishers, particularly the West Publishing Company and the Lawyers' Co-op Bancroft Whitney Publishing Company. Once a student becomes familiar with the features in one state, that knowledge can be easily applied to other states.

Finally, I would like to acknowledge a special debt to Professor Jean Love of the Law Faculty of the University of California at Davis for the perceptive insights on teaching legal research and analysis which she has generously shared with me and for her helpful critiques of prior drafts of this manual. I am also indebted to Professor Mortimer D. Schwartz, Librarian, Law Library, University of California at Davis for his patience, generosity, and counsel.

A. J. L.
Davis, California

CHAPTER I

SOME INTRODUCTORY MATTERS

A. Bibliographic Control and Organization of Law Books

1. The Accessibilty of American Law

There is no substantial body of literature in the history of the world that is as well indexed as American law. There are literally millions of appellate court decisions, court rules, constitutions, statutes, charters, ordinances, treaties, executive orders, proclamations, and administrative regulations—coming from the three branches of government at various local, state, and national levels and currently from fifty-one jurisdictions—that constitute the body of laws made during our two hundred years of sovereign history. Yet, despite this great bulk of law, there is an excellent chance that you could find one of these laws at any good sized law library—even if you only have a partial description of what you are looking for.

All of this law is so accessible for two reasons. First, it is elementary that if "*Ignorantia juris non excusat,*" then the government must make some effort to inform us of these laws that bind us. Second, the great size and wealth of this country, with its concomitant volume of legal business, have created a market which private publishers have entered, with some very sophisticated tools for legal research.

2. The Beginnings of Legal Publishing

Many of the currently used forms of legal literature that private individuals have devised have a very long history. Back in the reign of Edward I (1272-1307), some people (they may have been training themselves to be lawyers) started sitting in on trials, recording what happened, and what was said. These accounts were later collected in a series called the *Year Books.* From that time, in a virtually unbroken string, "law reporting" has continued in England, the United States, and the other common law countries to the present day.

It is presumed that it was an Englishman named Statham who first took it upon himself to produce a subject key to all of these cases that were accumulating in the fourteenth and fifteenth centuries. In 1490 his *Abridgment of the Year Books* was published. That abridgment was the forerunner of today's legal encyclopedias and digests.

During the reign of Edward III (1327-1377) the *Natura Brevium* and the *Novae Narrationes* were published. An accurate knowledge of the "writs" was vital in those days. If you did not know the right words, the court could not hear you. These two books collected the writs and provided commentaries and notes from cases in the *Year Books*. Today, it is the California (or other state) Continuing Education of the Bar, the Matthew Bender Co., or one of the other publishers that is producing these practical manuals for busy lawyers.

3. Automation

Many people, both in and outside the profession, have been struck by the obvious relevance of automated information retrieval to legal research. And, indeed, case and statutory retrieval systems have been in use in some jurisdictions (notably in New York, Pennsylvania, and Ohio) for several years. There is little doubt that in the long run all legal publishing and retrieval will be automated. Two factors are delaying the process. First, as has been pointed out, the present nonautomated techniques of publishing, supplementing, and indexing law, are relatively efficient. Secondly, the costs of automation in this field are enormous and neither government nor private industry want to invest the capital unless they are reasonably sure of a sufficient market. Published law, particularly court decisions, comprises a huge bulk of material which, it has been learned, must be entered full-text into any system and then supplemented and corrected on a daily basis. It must also be intensively indexed. Finally, many people with many different needs must be able to query the system from all over a state or even the entire United States.

4. Primary Sources, Search Books, and Secondary Sources; Title Pages

The first time you enter a good sized law library, you may feel overwhelmed by the great number and variety of books found there. If your livelihood is going to depend, to some extent, on a familiarity with all those books, the prospect may seem disheartening. There are some very simple notions, however, which can be learned in order to help organize this chaos of details within your mind.

For example, every law book falls into at least one of three categories: primary sources, search books, or secondary sources. Primary sources are those books containing *the text of the law.* Law comes from many origins. It comes from every branch, on every level, within every jurisdiction (states and federal) of our federal system. When laws are made, they are printed in books called primary sources.

They are printed in the chronological order in which they are made. Examples of primary sources are reporters (court decisions), session laws (legislative enactments), county ordinances, the *Federal Register* (regulations of federal administrative agencies), and *U.S. Treaties* and other *International Agreements*.

The difficulty with primary sources is the chronological arrangement. You need something that provides a subject approach and also something that separates the law currently in force from all the law that has been made over a long period of time. This is what search books do. Session laws, for example, are codified into books called codes (and various other names) which arrange all of the statutes that are currently in force by subject.*

The opinions from court decisions are abstracted. These abstracts are arranged by subject in a type of search book called a digest. Another search book for court-made law is called a citator. It will aid in determining what court decisions still have the force of law.

The third category of law books is secondary sources. Secondary sources provide expert comment, summary, explanation, synthesis, and criticism of the law. They include such materials as legal periodicals, textbooks, treatises, encyclopedias, dictionaries, looseleaf services, formbooks, and annotated reporters.

In addition to knowing the categories, there is one simple trick you can learn in order to identify the contents of many books in a law library: read the title page. Law books typically specify their contents and scope with a short, accurate statement on the title page. For example, the several hundred volume set of books called *Federal Supplement* might mean nothing to you until you scan the statement on the title page that reads, "Cases Argued and Determined in the United States District Court, United States Customs Court."

B. Special Characteristics of Law Books

1. They Are Designed for Lawyers and Judges – Not for Students and Scholars

A social scientist will turn to a law library to find the status of legalized abortion in the states of the United States. A lawyer will turn to a law library to find out if the Washington Joint Unified School District was liable when one of its temporary employees struck and caused damage to a stolen vehicle at night, during a storm that blew down the stop sign, at an intersection in a neighboring state, when the

*Actually codes (of statutes, ordinances, or administrative regulations) can also be regarded as primary materials since they also contain the text of the law.

employee was drunk and was using the school bus for his own purposes and without authority. The lawyer's research might take a couple of hours. The social scientist might spend a year at his task. (It surprises many people to learn that there is no single index to all the state laws.) Law books are practical tools designed to answer those very specific questions arising from that phenomenon which is the foundation of all law: a particular controversy between two people or organizations. Law books are not designed to answer general questions.

2. Citation to Authorities

a. Citation Form

You will not have to use any secondary law books for very long before realizing that legal writing is heavily annotated. Two sentences cannot be put together without citing authority. Authority of course means the law: cases, statutes, etc. This makes sense because no one wants to make decisions that effect life, liberty and property based merely on someone's word as to the legal effect of these decisions.

Unlike a great deal of other annotated writings, in law people actually do look up these cited authorities. Therefore, rules of citation form are critical to insure accuracy. The most widely recognized compilation of these rules is *A Uniform System of Citation,* The Harvard Law Review Association, 11th edition, 1967 ("Harvard White Book"). Throughout this manual, I have indicated the correct citation form after each type of law book discussed. These sample citations are based largely on the "White Book."

b. Binding and Persuasive Authority

When learning about legal authorities, two concepts which will need to be understood initially are binding versus persuasive authority and holding versus dictum. Binding authorities are those laws that are controlling in a certain situation. For example, if a person is being tried in California for an act allegedly committed in California and considered a crime under the California Penal Code—his attorney will want to cite favorable statutes and appellate court decisions which he feels he can convince the judge are applicable. Of course, he will look for California statutes and appellate decisions first because the trial judge would be bound by these authorities. If as sometimes happens, there are no statutes or cases that are strictly on point, or if the attorney is talking to an appellant bench and is seeking a change in the law, he may cite persuasive authorities. Such persuasive authorities could include decisions from other state courts, scholarly commentary in the law reviews or treaties, the opinions of the state attorney general, or even other state statutes in special cases.

c. Holding and Dictum

Holding and dictum refer to the authority of various statements in appellate court opinions. An appellate bench not only decides to affirm, reverse, modify, etc., the lower court's decision, but also writes an "opinion" that sets forth an analysis of the issues in the case and explains the reasons for the decision (see the chapter on Case Law). It is from a reading of the import of these opinions that holdings are determined. These holdings then become precedents (legal rules) for similar, subsequent cases. For example, the Supreme Court of the United States, in *Brown* v. *Board of Education of Topeka*, 347 U.S. 483 (1954), reversed the Federal District Court decisions and ruled that the racially segregated schools in certain districts in Kansas, South Carolina, Virginia, and Delaware were in violation of the equal protection clause of the Fourteenth Amendment. In the foregoing, the court was simply handing down a final adjudication on some related controversies between individuals and their school districts. As we all know, however, this case held and is precedent for the *rule of law* that any system of school segregation based solely on race is in violation of the equal protection laws of the Fourteenth Amendment. We also know that this is true even if the facilities are equal, because the court accepted it as fact that the Kansas facilities were equal.

During the course of the court's opinion, Chief Justice Warren discussed the historical background surrounding the adoption of the Fourteenth Amendment and made several statements to the effect that these historical sources are inconclusive on the question of what the drafters and ratifiers of the amendment intended it to mean ("At best, they [the historical sources] are inconclusive"). These statements are dicta (except insofar as they relate to education). One cannot cite the *Brown* case as holding that you cannot use historical sources to determine the intent of the framers of the Fourteenth Amendment. The full expression for this concept is *obiter dicta* which means incidental words.

3. Legal Supplementation

Since laws change constantly, law books must be featured to accomodate rapid supplementation. A strict rule of legal research is to always update! Check the dates of publication or coverage of any book you are using.

One method of supplementation that is peculiar to law books is the "pocket part." A pocket part is a paper bound pamphlet/booklet that inserts into a pocket on the inside back cover of the book it supplements. Other devices include booklets and pamphlets shelved after the volume or the set being up-dated, replacement volumes in a set, and looseleaf pages that replace prior pages.

C. Research Strategy

Your research will be much more fruitful and efficient if you adopt a strategy before starting any legal research project. Strategy means a determination ahead of time of what books you are going to use and what order you are going to use them in. Unfortunately, it is impossible to provide beginners with a model program that sets forth, step-by-step, how to do legal research. There are too many variables relating to the nature of legal problems, the sophistication of the researcher, the amount of time available, and the facilities of the particular law library. The three research strategy charts in appendix A, however, attempt to provide some overall orientation. The first chart assumes that you have some general knowledge of the area of the law being researched, including whether it is a state or federal matter; the second assumes you do not know the area of the law very well; and the third assumes that you have a special problem.

The real key to research strategy is to know the books. You cannot choose among options unless you know what they are. Knowing the books does not mean knowing all the details. You can be an excellent researcher even if you do not know that, " . . . a parallel conversion table in volume 21 of the First Decennial translates from the Century section numbers to the Decennial Key Numbers." However, you do have to know that when you want the regulations of the U.S. Equal Employment Opportunity Commission—you must go to the *Code of Federal Regulations.* For every title covered in this manual there are only three fundamental questions you must be able to answer: what does it contain, how is it indexed, and how is it supplemented? Moreover, there are not that many titles covered; besides, they all fall into a pattern based on the factors discussed *supra.* You will have the beginnings of a good research strategist if you can stand in the lobby of a law library with an outline in your head of the major sets of books which can be found inside that library.

There are also a few other notes on research strategy that would be helpful in the beginning. First, you must realize that "law" in the United States really means fifty-one different systems of law. Stop to think about which system's law books you want to go into. The distinction between state and federal is especially important. A second decision you often have to make is whether you are going to look for cases or for statutes. It is far too complex to explain here, but laws regulating some activities come from the legislatures and others from the courts and many from both. For example, the law on assault and battery is going to be found in court decisions while that on public utilities is largely found in statutes. When in doubt, check the statutes first. Lastly, do not neglect the secondary sources. At a minimum, they will supply you with the general orientation needed and the annotations will lead to the primary authorities which can be checked later in order to draw your own conclusions.

D. Law Libraries

There are several hundred medium to large sized law school or county law libraries in the United States which students and the general public may use. This is, of course, especially true if they are publicly supported. Smaller law libraries serving particular courts, governmental departments, or other specialized clientele and libraries supported by bar association fees will not be available. In any case, you will be much more welcome if you know your way around law books. One thing you should know is that all law libraries are noncirculating. A legal collection is like one big "reference room" collection; the books have to be used within the building. Of course, photocopiers have made it much easier for everyone to live with this rule.

CHAPTER II

STATUTORY LAW

A. Check the Statutes First!

There are no exact rules in legal research. One rule that comes close, however, is **check the statutes first.** Often when you have to do some research you do not know where to start. You do not know if there is any law on the subject. If there is some law, you do not know whether it comes from court decisions, statutes, administrative regulations or some other source or combination of sources. The best bet in such a situation is to see if there is a statute on point. There are at least two reasons for this. First, generally speaking, statutes are more "important" than cases, administrative regulations, and other sources of law. It is the legislative branch that has primary responsibility for making laws. The courts and the administrative agencies have no authority to alter the clear meaning of the statute's language. Often in research you will find that for a complete understanding of the law on one subject, you must consult statutes, cases, administrative regulations, and perhaps, even other sources. The starting point, however, is the statute itself. All else is merely interpretation and effectuation of the purposes of the statute. Of course, if there is a relevant constitutional provision, then it will take precedence and become the starting point for your research. A second reason for starting research with the statutes is that they are found in the most useful and time saving kinds of law books there are: annotated codes.

B. The Text of Statutes

1. Session Laws and Codes

Statutes are published in two different forms: chronological and codified (*i.e.*, arranged by subject). We will use California and the federal government for examples. Let us talk about the chronological form first.

a. Session Laws

Every year the California legislature passes laws. These laws are published annually in an official state publication entitled *Statutes and*

Amendments to the Codes. All the other states and the federal government publish their enactments in the same form. The enactments from Congress are published in a series of volumes called *United States Statutes at Large.* From state to state, these go under various names (*e.g., Laws of the State of . . . , Public and Local Acts of . . . , Acts and Resolves of . . . , etc.*) but the generic name for these books that contain, in chronological order, the enactments of legislatures is **Session Laws.** In California each enactment is given a chapter number in consecutive order as it is signed by the governor.

For Congress you need only be interested, for now, in the "public laws" section of the *Statutes at Large.* Each enactment is given a public law number in consecutive order as it is signed by the president.

b. Codes (annotated and unannotated)*

I think the best way of explaining what the codes and annotated codes are is by proving that if there were no such things, somebody would have had to invent them. Imagine how you would go about doing research in California statutory law if all you had were the session laws. In order to find out what the California legislature has said on any one subject you might conceivably have to start with the latest volume of the session laws and look at every volume back to the year 1850. This way you would be sure to have the full text of all related laws on the subject along with all of their amendments and repeals. Even then, you would not be through because it is generally not enough to have just the text of the statutes. You would also need to find out if the courts have interpreted any of that text.

Having gone through this imaginary and painful experience, it would have become apparent that there was a need for a set of books that:

1. arranged all of the statutes by subject
2. deleted the repealed statutes
3. inserted all amendments and additions
4. provided a single index to all subjects
5. had a system for frequent supplementation
6. provided citations to cases that had considered any of the statutes.

Thanks to free enterprise and law book publishers, we have been rescued from this drudgery. Annotated codes do all of the above and

*I have used the term "code(s)" because that is what they are called on the federal level and in California. Other states may call these books or sets of books by other names, for example: *McKinney's Consolidated Laws of New York Annotated, West's Oklahoma Statutes Annotated, Oregon Revised Statutes, South Dakota Compiled Laws.* In lawyers' parlance they are often just called "statutes."

unannotated codes do the first five. There are annotated and unannotated codes for federal legislation and for almost all of the states. (All states will have their statutes in at least one form.)

An unannotated code should be used when you are principally interested in the language of a statute, or when you want to see the relationships between a sequence of statutes. An annotated code should be used when you want to research the legislative history and judicial interpretation of a statute. Annotated codes typically contain historical information on the enactment of a statute, citations to judicial opinions construing the statute, and references to secondary sources which are relevant to the statute (*e.g.*, citations to encyclopedias, law review articles, and form books).

Codes are arranged by subject; that is what "codify" means. In California, all statutes appear in one of the following codes:

Agriculture
Business and Professions
Civil
Civil Procedure
Commercial
Corporations
Education
Elections
Evidence
Financial
Fish and Game
Government
Harbors and Navigation
Health and Safety
Insurance
Labor
Military and Veterans
Penal
Probate
Public Resources
Public Utilities
Revenue and Taxation
Streets and Highways
Unemployment Insurance
Vehicle
Water
Welfare and Institutions

Codes are always indexed through a general index to the entire set and sometimes have separate individual volume or title indexes as well. A table of contents normally appears at the beginning of each new section. (In California, the table of contents is called "Analysis.") The table of contents approach is only for those who are familiar with the logical structure of the law and can go from major heading to subheading, to sub-subheading, etc.,to find the specific point of law in question. Unless you know the area of the law you are looking into quite well, it is best to start with the general index. (See pages 17-19 for "Steps in using annotated codes.")

The method of keeping codes and annotated codes current varies. In California, for example, there are "pocket parts" in the back of each bound volume which bring the bound volumes up to date from the time they were published to the beginning of the current year. Pamphlets which are published periodically during the current year reproduce the current session laws (*Advance Legislative Service*) or supplement the annotated codes (*Cumulative Pamphlets*).

In California, there are two sets of annotated codes: *Deering's California Codes Annotated* and *West's Annotated California Codes.* They are both good. The numbering system is the same. For example, the two citations for the definition of burglary in California are:

> California Penal Code § 459 (Deering 1971)
> California Penal Code § 459 (West 1970)

The date is the year of publication of the volume which contains § 459 of the Penal Code.

At the federal level, there are three sets of codes:

1. *United States Code:* An official publication of the United States Government; it is not annotated.
2. *United States Code Annotated:* This is the most popular federal code service. It is published by West Publishing Co.
3. *United States Code Service:* This is the other nonofficial federal code service. It is gradually replacing a former service called *Federal Code Annotated.* The set will be difficult to use until replacement is complete.

All three federal code sets use the same numbering system. If you were in the Army and wanted to know your worth in terms of square feet of floor space, you would want to consult the following statute:

> In the construction of family quarters from appropriated funds for members of the Army, the following are the maximum limitations on net floor area for each unit:

Grade	*Square Feet*
General officer	2,100
Colonel	1,670
Major or lieutenant colonel	1,400
Officer below major	1,250
Enlisted member	1,080

The various citations for the above statute are:

> 10 USC § 4774(a) (1970)
> 10 USCA § 4774(a) (1959)
> 10 FCA § 4774(a) (1965)

The dates in parentheses indicate the date of publication or copyright of the particular volume of the respective sets in which title 10, section

4774(a) is found. The general rule is that you cite to the official USC only.

Correct Citation Form

Federal

(session law)—Sugar Act Amendment of 1971, Pub. L. no. 92-138, § 3, 85 Stat. 379

(code)—31 USC § 691 (1970)

State

(session law)—Ch. 867, § 1, [1945] Cal. Stat. 1626

(code)—Cal. Code Civ. Pro. § 437c (West, 1954).

2. Local Statutes (city and county ordinances)

City and county ordinances also follow the pattern of state and federal statutes. They are numbered and printed in consecutive order as they are passed by the city council or county board of supervisors. These separate printings of the ordinances are not generally published, however, and what you will be using will be the codes of city or county ordinances. The codes are arranged under major titles like the state and federal codes and they are generally indexed. They are not annotated.

The only problem in using local ordinances is finding them. Many local communities are negligent in having their ordinances printed and published promptly. Your only recourse may be to go to the county office or city hall to see a copy.

Correct Citation Form

The Code of the City of Davis, California, § 28-1 (1971)

C. The Steps in Using Annotated Codes Are As Follows

1. *Find the set of codes for your jurisdiction: federal or state.*
2. *Turn to the multivolumed general index at the end of the set.* Using indexes to law books is apt to be one of the more frustrating experiences of legal research. The problem will be to guess how the complier indexed the material you are looking for. One thing that will help you is to know that every day factual words as well as legal terms are used. For example, on a certain page in an index to the California codes, I can find "Highway users' tax fund," "Hive syrum," "Hoboes," "Hokey-pokey," and "Holders in due course."

3. *Find the entry in the general index and notice that it will give you a reference to a code and section in the main body of the set* (*e.g.*, FG 12300 = Fish and Games Code, § 12300).
4. *Get the correct code volume and turn to the referenced section.* The first thing you will see is a heading in dark type that has been made up by the compiler. All of the language after that heading, in ordinary type, down to the historical notes (*viz.*, "Legislative History," "Former Revisions," etc.) is *the text of the law.* It is word-for-word the same language that was enacted into law by the legislature. (You could verify this by referring to the historical notes to get the references to the session laws and then going to the correct annual volume of the session laws.)
5. *Read the text of the law carefully.* (See pages 19-25, "Interpreting the Text of Statutes.")
6. *Read the annotations.*

   Later on you will learn more about the role of the courts and some other institutions (*e.g.*, Attorney General) in interpreting the text of statutes. It is enough for now to know that in our system of jurisprudence, the courts have a fair measure of discretion in *interpreting* the text and constitutionality of statutes that they are asked to apply to particular situations when they are deciding cases. Therefore, you will want to read those cases similar to yours that have applied the section of the codes you are interested in. What you find (under a heading like "Notes of Decisions") are digests of points of law discussed in cases that have cited the section in question. These are also called headnotes, squibs, or syllabi. The digest is followed by a citation to the case. The origin of these is explained later in the text under "Digests."

   The annotations will often also include cross references to other code sections, references to attorney general opinions that have interpreted the section in question, and collateral references to relevant secondary legal materials (textbooks, encyclopedias, and law review articles).
7. *Check the "pocket part."*

   If you looked at the copyright date of any particular volume you would often find that it was published several years earlier. Obviously, the publishers have supplemented that volume since the user needs to know the *current* state of the law. Most codes are supplemented by pocket parts. They come out annually and are inserted in a pocket inside the back cover. The pocket part uses the same numbering system as the bound volume, so you can check your original code and section number reference there. The pocket part will tell if the language of the statute you have read in the bound volume has been affected by subsequent legislative activity (added to, repealed, or otherwise amended) generally through December of the prior year. It will also update the annotations to that particular section.

8. *Update further.*
   The pocket part will bring you up to the beginning of the current year. During the current year the publisher will issue soft bound booklets that are shelved at the end of the entire set. There will be two kinds:

   a. Advance legislative service. This will give the text of new statutes as they are passed by the legislature (*i.e.*, session laws). It will contain cummulative tables that will take you from your code section number to the relevant session law.
   b. Annotation supplement (sometimes called "Cummulative Pamphlets" or "Later Case Service"). This will give digests of any recent cases that have interpreted the code section. The advance sheets of the case reporters (see page 45, "Reporters—Advance Sheets") also contain tables of "statutes construed" which can give references to later cases.

   Sometimes another type of supplement may be found. It is generally called a "cummulative supplement" which will be a semi-permanently bound booklet that will sit on the shelf next to the hard bound volume it supplements. These are used when the pocket part has become too fat to insert in the bound volume and the publishers have not yet published a replacement to the bound volume.

   The trick with supplementing *all* legal research is to check the dates of coverage of any bound volume, pocket part, booklet, pamphlet, or looseleaf page you are using. It you read these carefully and look all around on the shelves nearby, your research should be complete and up to date.

D. Interpreting the Text of Statutes

When doing statutory research, the first job is to read the text carefully. The language is very deliberate; each word counts. What does the statute *precisely* say regarding your situation? Are there any ambiguities that can help you or hurt you? The second job is to go to other sources, official and unofficial, that can help you and the court interpret the statute. As indicated earlier, the main finding tools for these other sources of interpretation are the annotations in an annotated code. Below are other books you will have to be familiar with in order to do statutory research.

1. Reporters

These books will be covered more thoroughly in the chapter on case law. At this point, however, something should be said about reporters because you will encounter them in your use of annotated codes. The most important sources of statutory interpretation are the reports of cases that have applied sections of statutes to particular situations. These interpretations will be binding or persuasive authority depending on the level of the court and the jurisdiction.

When an appellate court decides a case, it not only announces its decision to affirm, reverse, modify, etc., the decision of the lower court, but it also generally publishes an "opinion" which explains why it reached its decision. These opinions are published chronologically in books called reporters.

Correct Citation Form (cases)

Cases are cited by:

1. name of case
2. volume number of reporter
3. name of reporter
4. page of reporter
5. date of decision

Example:

Park v. *Franciscus*, 194 Cal. 284 (1924)

2. Attorney Generals' Opinions

The attorney general is the government's lawyer. One of his or her functions is to provide written opinions on questions of law submitted by government officials. Typically, this includes legislators, top members of the executive branch, district attorneys, and county counsels. These opinions, which are published, are recognized as strong persuasive authority by the courts.

Generally, you do not directly search for an attorney general opinion when you are looking for authority. There is no current index or other specific finding tool to these opinions. States, from time to time, will publish cumulative indexes but they are seldom up to date. Primarily, you will find references to these while using the annotated statutes.

Correct Citation Form

15 Op. Cal. Att'y Gen. 100 (1950)

3. Uniform Laws

Around the turn of the century there was considerable concern over what seemed to be an unnecessary, inconvenient, and uneconomic diversity in state laws. Two private, national organizations of outstanding lawyers, judges, and teachers came into being at that time to deal with the problem. The American Law Institute concerned itself with promoting uniformity in court made law and produced "Restatements" (see p. 77). The National Conference of Commissioners on Uniform States Laws did the same for legislation and produced "Uniform Laws." The products of both groups are highly respected but are *only advisory* to state courts and legislatures.

The National Conference is composed of representatives from each state (generally three) who are appointed by the governors. Through a long, deliberate process of tentative drafts, review, and rewriting, a "Uniform Law" is eventually drafted and can be recommended to all state legislatures for adoption. If one or more legislators introduce the uniform law as a bill it will then go through the usual process of hearings, reports, debates, amendments, and so forth for eventual passage or nonpassage as another state law.

The most important of all the uniform laws is the Uniform Commercial Code which has been adopted by almost all states. California's version of it can be found in either Deering's or West's annotated codes. There are also over a hundred other uniform laws. They are found in two sets: *Uniform Laws Annotated* and *Uniform Laws Annotated, Master Edition.* The *Master Edition* is gradually superseding the older edition and presently contains all of the most important acts. It is well annotated. The most important annotations are the explanatory notes or comments prepared by the Commissioners themselves and the citations to interpreting court decisions. These notes would be good persuasive authority if you were researching a state law that was derived from one of the Uniform Laws.

Correct Citation Form

Uniform Narcotic Drug Act § 20

4. Secondary Sources

Primary sources are those law books that provide the official text of the law (statutes, cases, administrative regulations). Secondary sources provide summaries, commentaries, explanations, or criticisms of the law. Examples of secondary sources are legal encyclopedias, law reviews, textbooks, practice books, and looseleaf services. These books are dealt with more thoroughly later. They must at least be mentioned at this point, however, because of their relevance to statutory research. Often, the easiest, quickest and smartest way to do statutory or any kind of legal research is to let some expert spell it all out for you in print. This is particularly true when you are dealing with an unfamiliar area of the law or when you do not have the time to do it all yourself. Of course, there is a risk in allowing someone else to interpret the text of statutes and court opinions for you, especially since your particular problem is almost always unique in some respects. You have to weigh these factors yourself. Legal research, however, is not academic research. A client cannot afford to finance an attorney's desire to satisfy his intellectual curiosity through scholarly searching.

5. Legislative History*

Frequently the disposition of a case is determined by the meaning given to some statutory language. The basic rule of statutory construction applied by the courts is the "plain meaning rule." That is, the court will effectuate the assumed intent of the legislature by construing the statute according to the most common meaning ascribed to the language used. Often, however, the meaning may not be very plain or one of the parties might present some cogent evidence of legislative intent that may not be apparent from the language. It is in these cases that the court will go outside the language of the statute itself for evidence of legislative intent. The court will turn to a legislative history.

a. The Legislative Process

Legislative history refers to those documents produced as a part of the statute enacting process. The basic outline of this process, which a student of law books should know, is as follows:

1. A bill is introduced. (**Bills** are numbered and printed.)
2. It is assigned to a committee. (It may die here or anywhere else along the line.)

*This handbook will only concern itself with federal legislative history. Only Congress regularly prints all of the legislative documents. Very few of the documents are available on a state level. Some research can be done, however, particularly in California and New York. California bills are all printed, but hearings, reports, and debates are often not available. You will probably need the help of a documents librarian at a law or general university library for help in this area.

3. Committee hearings may be held. (**Hearings** are printed under the name of the committee.)
4. It may be reported out of committee. (**Reports** are numbered and printed.)
5. There may be debate on the floor of the legislature. (**Debates** are printed and dated.)
6. Finally, the bill, perhaps after several amendments, may be passed by the legislature and signed by the chief executive. (**Statutes** or **session laws** are numbered and printed.)

Your research task in doing a legislative history is to go to an index which will give the references (numbers, names of committees, sessions of the legislature, dates, etc.) needed for any one bill or statute, then obtain the documents, and finally apply a lawyer's analytical skills in interpreting these documents.

b. CCH Congressional Index

One of the most widely used indexes to the federal legislative process is published by Commerce Clearing House and is called the *CCH Congressional Index*. The chart and the steps below indicate how this tool is used:

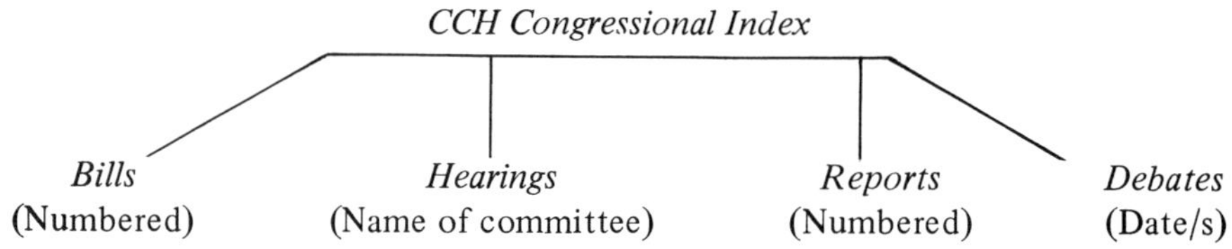

Steps

1. Go to the "Subject Index" to find the House or Senate Bill number.
2. Go to "House Bills" or "Senate Bills" to find the short title of the bill and the name of the committee to which it was assigned.
3. Go to "Status of House Bills" or "Status of Senate Bills" where you will find out what has happened to a bill *if* it has at least gone far enough for hearings to be held.
4. Having taken steps 1, 2, and 3, you can now write down the following information:
   a. House or Senate Bill Number
   b. Name of the committee to which it was assigned
   c. House or Senate Report Number
   d. Dates of debate or other action on the House or Senate floor

5. With the information gathered in step 4 you can obtain a complete legislative history from a documents librarian. A complete legislative history will include the following documents:
   a. Printings of the various amended versions of the bill
   b. Transcript of committee hearings
   c. The committee report
   d. Debates from the *Congressional Record*

c. Congressional Information Service

Another comprehensive Congressional indexing service you will encounter at libraries is called the *Congressional Information Service.* It has abstracting and full text features, in addition to being an index. The *Congressional Information Service* is composed of three parts: the *CIS Index,* the *CIS Annual* and the *CIS Microfiche Library.* Not all libraries subscribe to the complete service. The *CIS Index* is an excellent index to hearings, reports, and other Congressional committee documents but will not give records of bills introduced but not heard in committee, nor will it record debates on the floor. It also does not provide status tables of all introduced bills as does the *CCH Congressional Index.* Current status tables are necessary when you want to follow a bill's progress (or lack of such) through Congress. An added feature of the *CIS Index* is that it provides you with abstracts of the committee documents that it indexes. As an index to hearings, it is superior to the *CCH Congressional Index.*

The *CIS Annual* cummulates the abstracts and indexes of the *CIS Index* and gives references to the documents you would refer to in doing a legislative history of enacted laws.

The *CIS Microfiche Library* contains the actual text (in microfiche) of those documents which are indexed in the *CIS Index.* If the library you are using is not a federal depository library (which receives these Congressional documents in hard copy, free of charge from the government), it may subscribe to the *CIS Microfiche Library.*

d. U.S. Code: Congressional and Administrative News

This set is a very useful shortcut to researching legislative history arguments. In this publication, each session of congress is basically divided in two parts: "Laws" and "Legislative history."

The "Laws" part is simply the text of the statutes passed during that session (*i.e.,* the session laws). The statutes are published much earlier here than in *Statutes at Large.*

The primary use of this set is the "Legislative history" part which generally publishes the text of some of the committee reports. Citations to all of the reports and to the *Congressional Record* (for floor debates) are also given. This is far from being a complete legislative history, but it does give the text of one or two of the most important documents in a convenient form. You will notice that both the "Laws" and the "Legislative histories" are arranged by public law number and have references to each other in italics right after the name of the act.

e. How Are Legislative Documents Used in Interpreting Statutes?

It is beyond the scope of this book to answer this question in any great detail. Below, however, some of the possible uses of each of these documents are briefly discussed:

Bills: As a bill is amended during the legislative process it is reprinted. Each new printing will contain the new language. These progressive additions, deletions, and alterations in the language are direct evidence of deliberate thinking. For example, if a bill originally excluded registered pharmacists from its intended coverage, but such exclusionary language was dropped in the final enactment, a good argument could be made that the legislature intended to *include* registered pharmacists.

Hearings: These are transcripts of testimony offered by invited experts on the subject of the proposed legislation. They can be useful in indicating what information the legislature presumably had when it enacted a particular statute.

Reports: If a bill is not "buried" in a committee, the committee will report it out to the full legislature along with a recommendation that it pass or not pass. This is the most obviously useful of all the legislative documents in proving intent. A report will summarize the provisions of a bill and give the committee's explanation of its purpose(s).

Debates: You have probably heard of the *Congressional Record* which is a daily transcript of what was said on the floor of the House and Senate. Statements by legislators for or against passage of a bill can often be used to indicate how they were interpreting the meaning of its language.

E. Other Tools for Statutory Research

1. Shepards (statutes)

When you have found a statute that is on point, the next task is to determine its current status. In other words it is important to know whether or not the language you are looking at has been subsequently amended or repealed by the legislature and whether or not it has been considered by the courts. As you have already learned, this is precisely what is done by the annotated codes along with their pocket parts and pamphlet supplements. It is my opinion that the annotated codes do a thorough job of this and are more convenient than Shepards. Some people prefer Shepards, however, and on rare occasion it can be demonstrated that a reference found in Shepards cannot be found in the annotated codes.

Shepards is a citation service. In other words it tells if something you are looking at (a section of the statutes or a case) has been mentioned (cited) since it was first published. Let us consider § 834(a) of the California Penal Code which states, in general, that you may not resist an arrest if you know that you are being arrested by a peace officer. If you checked the California Codes, you would find out that this section was enacted in 1957. Shepards could then tell whether the California Legislature or any court had ever cited § 834(a), which is another way of saying that Shepards could tell if the legislature had amended, repealed or added to it or if the courts had held it constitutional, unconstitutional, or interpreted its meaning.

a. Locate the Shepards for the jurisdiction in which you are interested.
b. For some jurisdictions, particularly the federal, there are many different Shepards volumes which cover not only statutes but also the various reporter series, administrative agencies, and other matters. The volumes you want will probably say: "Constitution, Code, Statutes . . . " on the back. Make sure that you not only have the basic bound volume, but also all of its supplements. Generally there will be a red and sometimes also a white soft bound booklet. Find those that say "Statutes." Check the dates of coverage for each of the hard and soft bound parts to make sure there is a complete set with no gaps. The latest supplement should cover up to within at least the last two months.
c. Locate the code section you are interested in. In California, code titles (*e.g.*, Penal Code, Code of Civil Procedure, etc.) will be found at the tops of the pages. Section numbers are in heavy type throughout each page. Under each section number there will be a list of citations to statutes, cases, attorney general opinions and other published matters that have cited your code section. Some coded letters may also be found preceding these citations.

d. Turn to the first few pages of the volume you are using and locate the tables entitled "Abbreviations-Analysis." They will explain what the citations and coded letters mean.
e. Check all the supplements.

The above explanation does not cover all of the problems you might run into in using Shepards for statutory research, but it does illustrate the most typical use. *Shepards United States Citations* for federal statutes is the same as for California except that code titles are listed at the top of the page by number only (*e.g.*, "T.20") and not by name. Both California and federal Shepards have a separate section for uncodified statutes.

2. Popular Name Tables

People who find their references to statutes through the news media often have need of these tables. When the only reference you have is the "Kathy Fiscus Act" or the "Patman-Robinson Act"—a popular name table will need to be used. The most complete listing is *Shepard's Acts and Cases by Popular Names, Federal and State.*

Popular name tables are also found in the California annotated statutes (West: under "popular name laws" in the index; Deering's: scattered throughout the index under the individual popular names), as well as many other state annotated statutes: the *United States Code Annotated,* and the *United States Code Service.*

CHAPTER III

ADMINISTRATIVE AGENCY LAW

A. What Are Administrative Agencies? How Do They Make Law?

Usually, laymen are reasonably familiar with the theory and process of legislative lawmaking. Judicial lawmaking causes a few problems and is discussed under "Case Law." The concept of administrative agency lawmaking is least familiar. For that reason it would be good to set forth some basic notions first.

The power to make law rests ultimately with the people. We, the people, have adopted a constitution which sets forth, in broad terms, the machinery of government and indicates the law making powers of each branch. The legislative branch has found that because of the great scope and complexity of its lawmaking powers, it must delegate the detailed exercise of those powers to boards, commissions, bureaus, departments, and so forth. Congress and state legislatures create administrative agencies by statute and define the scope and function of each agency. Within the confines of that definition, the agency makes rules, adjudicates, issues licenses, distributes money, investigates, prosecutes, mediates, and exercises whatever other powers the legislature felt were necessary for the agency to carry out a legislative purpose. The executive department also delegates in much the same way.

In this chapter we will be concerned with how and where administrative agencies publish their rules and regulations. Where do you find the rules of the California Department of Alcoholic Beverage Control on retention of a liquor license? Who is eligible for food stamps? Where do you find postal regulations? What rules does the State Division of Consumer Services have to control deceptive advertising?

B. The Overall Pattern of Publication

Before going into any detail on the individual publications used to find administrative law, it will be very helpful to scan the overall pattern first. This can be seen in the following chart:

Tools for Finding Administrative Rules and Regulations

State	Federal
California Administrative Register	*Federal Register*
California Administrative Code	*Code of Federal Regulations* (*CFR*)
California Blue Book	*United States Government Manual*

The pattern with administrative regulations is much the same as with statutes. If you will remember, statutes first appear in chronological order as they are passed and signed into law (session laws) and later codified. Administrative law also first appears in chronological order (*California Administrative Register* and *Federal Register*) and later is codified (*California Administrative Code* and *Code of Federal Regulations*). The *California Blue Book* and the *United States Government Manual* describe the organization and functions of the government agencies that are producing these rules and regulations.

C. The *California Administrative Register;* the *California Administrative Code*

In actual use, you will not see the *Register* itself. As soon as these weekly, numbered releases come to a subscriber, they are filed directly in the *Administrative Code* under the title amended, added to, or deleted. The *Code* is arranged under twenty-five titles or subjects. If you remember statutory codes, you would expect a general index at the end of the twenty-five titles. However, they never got around to doing that. There is no general index to the whole set. The finding tool you will use most is at the beginning of the first volume. It is called the "Table of Titles and Chapter Headings." This should get you to the right title; once you are there, each title has a detailed table of contents in the front. Sometimes there are indexes at the back of titles or parts of titles. Another finding aid located at the beginning of the first volume is the "Alphabetical Index of Agencies."

At the top of each page you will see a register number and date. If these pages had been filed in date and number order, you would have the *California Administrative Register*.

D. Other States

Only a dozen or so states publish a codification of their administrative regulations. For the remaining states, the appropriate agency must be contacted. Typically, each agency will have a pamphlet to distribute containing its rules and regulations.

Since earliest times, governmental entities have been remiss in meeting their obligation to provide prompt and convenient publication of their laws—either to those who must administer them or those affected by them. The only reason so much legal documentation and literature is available is that there has been a market for statutory codes, reporters, citators, legal encyclopedias, and so forth, and private publishers have stepped in. Publishers have not felt that they could sell enough subscriptions to state administrative codes to cover the high costs of printing, compiling, editing, indexing, and supplementing.

Correct Citation Form
13 Cal. Ad. Code § 100.00 (4-8-72)

E. The *Federal Register;* the *Code of Federal Regulations* (*CFR*)

1. Historical Background

Back in 1935 there was the case of *Panama Refining Co.,* v. *Ryan,* 293 US 388, in which the constitutionality of a regulation of the Department of the Interior was being challenged. The case went through a trial and reached the oral argument stage in the U.S. Supreme Court before someone found out that the regulation in question had been revoked by the government before the action had ever even commenced. Neither the plaintiff oil companies, the defendant enforcement officials, nor the courts were aware of this revocation. That year, in response to such a ridiculous state of affairs, Congress enacted the Federal Register Act. Basically the act provides that all rules, regulations, and procedures of the executive branch which will affect more than one person must be published in the *Federal Register.* This act and its subsequent amendments also provide for publication of the *Code of Federal Regulations* (*CFR*) and the *United States Government Manual.* CFR is a codification of what has appeared in the *Federal Register.*

2. Steps in Researching Federal Administrative Regulations

a. Check under the subject in the "General Index" volume and its supplements at the end of the *Code of Federal Regulations* (*CFR*). It will refer you to a title and section (or part) number in the main set.
b. Go to the main set. It is first organized under numbered titles, then by part, and then by section (*e.g.,* CFR 7 § 55.160 means

title 7, part 55, section 160). After reading the text of the regulation, note the revision date that is printed on the front cover. That date tells from what point forward you have to check for changes.

c. Go to the latest "List of CFR Sections Affected" (located on the shelf after the "General Index") and check under the title, part, and section number in which you are interested. If there are any changes, the "List" will refer you to the page in the *Federal Register* for the year that printed the changes. Note the date on the front cover of the "List." That date tells what later "Lists of CFR Sections Affected" must be checked.
d. Go to where the *Federal Register* is shelved. The latest issue of each month will have a "Cumulative List of Parts Affected." Check each of these lists to update what you did in step c. Again, if there are changes, a reference to a page number in the *Federal Register* will be given.
e. Find the text of the changes in the referenced pages of the *Federal Register.* The *Federal Register* comes out almost daily and the pages are numbered consecutively for an entire year.

3. Finding the Regulation When You Have the Statute: Getting from USC to CFR

A very useful table is found in the "Finding Aids" volume of CFR. "Table 1—Parallel Table of Statutory Authorities and Rules, . . . lists all sections of the United States Code . . . which are cited as rule-making authority for currently effective rules codified in the Code of Federal Regulations, or which are noted as being interpreted or applied by those rules." In other words, if you have been looking in the federal statutes you could take your USC or USCA citations (remember, they are both the same) and go to this table to see what rules have been made under the statute.

***Correct Citation Form** (**Federal Administrative Regulations**)*

29 CFR § 1607.3 (1972)
38 Fed. Reg. 12333 (1970)

F. The *California Blue Book;* the *United States Government Manual*

One of the difficulties of doing research in administrative law is the complexity of the organizational structure of the executive branch. We often do not know what agencies exist and what their functions are. It is frequently not enough to get the text of the regulations. What to a mere citizen seems to be a single activity, the government will view as being multifaceted and regulated by a number of agencies. For example, you cannot understand the federal government's ambivalent attitude toward recreational use of public land unless you know that the National Park Service is under the Interior Department and the National Forest Service is under the Agricultural Department, and that these two departments have differing and sometimes conflicting roles.

These organizational guides will generally list for each agency the staff, addresses, functions, organizational structure, and statutory authority. Both have good indexes. My favorites in the *United States Government Manual* are "The Center for Short-Lived Phenomena" and the "American Battle Monuments Commission." (During the Watergate difficulties, the listing of "The White House Office" served as a convenient "cast of characters.")

The *United States Government Manual* comes out yearly; the *California Blue Book* comes out every four years with each new administration. California also publishes a biennial "Roster" and an annual telephone directory which, of course, will have more current information on names, addresses, and telephone numbers.

G. Other States

All states, with the possible exception of Montana, have a state government manual with coverage similar to that indicated for California and the federal government. They are put out under varying names (*e.g.*, "register," "blue book," "directory," "guide," "manual," "year book," "roster," "almanac," and "handbook"). Most are published biennially and therefore some of the information can be out of date.

CHAPTER IV

CASE LAW

A. Reporters

1. The Common Law System

There are two major legal systems in the Western world: the common law system and the civil law system. Civil law is a development from the Roman codes and is founded on an assumption that all law comes from a legislative body. The civil law codes of European and other countries (notably Japan) are designed to cover every situation governed by law. In England, things happened differently . . .

In the late Middle Ages, when English law began its development in relative isolation from continental influences, the practice arose of writing down accounts of the proceedings and the reasoning applied at court trials. These accounts came to be used as precedents when similar cases came up later. Laziness, consistency, and an inclination to value real life experience over bloodless logic dictated such a system. Over the centuries since then, England has been unique in that a great body of law has been produced through this process of recording precedents. The technical name for the rule of applying precedents is *stare decisis*. *Stare decisis* may be defined as:

> The fundamental rule of the common law system whereby a court will hold itself bound to apply the same legal rules, in the same way, to a factual situation brought before it (or a superior court) applied in the past to essentially the same factual situation.
>
> Exception: the highest appellate courts will alter precedents when it is apparent to the current membership of the court that changed conditions in society or greater enlightenment so demand.

2. The Courts Make Law

Theoretically the judiciary is regarded as that branch of government which *applies* rules of law to conflicts between governmental units and/or private citizens. In fact, in common law countries, the courts play a large role in *making* these rules of law. This occurs in three areas:

a. Continual development of the common law

b. Interpreting statutes

c. Ruling on the constitutionality of governmental action

Reported decisions are an important source of law because much of our law has been developed exclusively by the courts through the centuries. Precedents in California, for example, go back not only to the state's first decisions in 1850 but, so far as they are applicable to the California situation, to the whole body of English common law. Section 22.2 of the California Civil Code provides:

> The common law of England, so far as it is not repugnant to or inconsistent with the Constitution of the United States, or the Constitution or laws of this State, is the rule of decision in all the courts of this State.

Most other states have similar provisions in their statutes.

Aside from those rules of law that have been developed exclusively by the courts, the courts have an equally important lawmaking role in interpreting legislation. Statutes are often couched in such general language that their actual effect on the activity being regulated cannot be determined until the courts are called upon to apply the language to actual controversies.

For example, you may know from general news reports that "class actions" are a significant, relatively new legal development. It is a procedure that permits a large, identifiable group of people who have suffered an alleged common harm to bring a single action. It is most often used in situations where it would not be worth the legal costs for the individual to sue on his own. The statutory language which currently permits class actions in California was enacted back in 1872. Because of varying interpretations of this language by the courts, however, over the past one hundred years the actual rule of law set down by § 382 of the Code of Civil Procedure has evolved from being a seldom used, narrow, and technical rule permitting "representative" actions to a major tool of legal relief to groups of people in civil rights, environmental and consumer protection areas. The courts' power to *interpret* legislation has always been construed liberally. In fact, they *make* a great deal of law in the process.

The last of the major functions of the courts is in determining that the government acts in accordance with its constitution. Again, as with interpreting legislation, the courts make a great deal of law in the process of applying the language of constitutional provisions to actual situations. The Supreme Court of the United States has developed a large body of law while "interpreting" that relatively short document known as the Constitution of the United States. State courts are also engaged in the same process.

3. Court Reports

The rules of law being made by the courts are found in their published *opinions* (also called "reports" or "cases"). Opinions are the written explanations of appellate courts for why they affirmed, reversed, modified, and so forth, the holding of the court or courts below. The court explains what rules of law apply to the issues raised by the appeal. Opinions are found in books called *reporters.* Reporters contain the text of opinions, case after case, in rough chronological order, as they are handed down.

If you now have some very preliminary understanding of how court opinions make law and how law coming from this source relates to law coming from other sources, you know why law libraries have thousands of volumes of reporters. It remains to go into some necessary details of the physical form and arrangement of these reports and the volumes of reporters they are found in.*

Get out a reporter volume and note the following elements in the report of any case:

a. *Title.* (*e.g., Haskins* v. *Morgan.*) This is also sometimes called "Name of the case."
b. *Docket number.* (*e.g.,* Civ. 1373).
c. *The name of the court.*
d. *The date* of the decision.
e. *Summary* of the case. This is also called a "syllabus." It is a short paragraph recounting what happened "below" and how the present appellate court holds.
f. *Headnotes.* These are also called "squibs" or "digests." They are summaries of the points of law stated in the opinion. They are written by commercial editors or by court reporters who more or less mechanically extract supposed statements of law found in the opinion. They include both holding and dictum.** Their primary function is to serve as the basis for a case-finding system known as digests (which will be covered later) and for annotated statutes. Occasionally, it is helpful to glance over the headnotes to get some idea of what the case is about before actually reading the opinion.
g. *The names of the attorneys.*

*The terminology used by lawyers is not always consistent. The author will refer to a report as the printed record of an individual case (these are also called "opinions" or "cases") and a reporter as the bound volume or volumes that contain the reports.

**Holdings are expressed or implied declarations by a court, relating to a rule of law or the interpretation of a rule of law, that were deemed necessary in order to decide the case. All other statements in an opinion are dicta. Only holdings are precedents. A court can only create precedents (*i.e.,* make law) in the process of deciding actual controversies.

h. *The Opinion.* The opinion always starts with the name of the justice who has written it. This is the official document. Here is where the law is found. The major portion of a student's three years in law school is spent in analyzing these opinions in order to determine what principles of law they are precedents for.
i. *The Order.* (*e.g.*, "Judgment is affirmed.")
j. The names of the other *concurring justices.*
k. *Dissenting Opinion* (if any). Nothing in a dissenting opinion can be cited as precedent (binding authority); however, it may be used as persuasive authority, especially if the court is fairly evenly divided.
l. The names of the other *dissenting justices* (if any).

4. The Pattern of Law Reporting in the United States (The chart on p. 43)

At first you may feel overwhelmed by the many different law reporters in a law library. If certain underlying factors are learned, however, you will soon be able to see an overall pattern that will make it much easier to learn the coverage of the individual reporters.

One of these underlying factors, of course, is our federal system which gives us reporters covering state and federal courts.

Another factor is the distinction between official and unofficial reporters. Most, but not all, states publish their own court opinions. The federal government, you will notice, only publishes the opinions of the United States Supreme Court. These official versions must be cited and they contain the official text. The unofficial versions are more widely used, however, and the text of the opinion is word-for-word the same as that in the official version.

With the exception of the Lawyers' Co-op Publishing Company's *U.S. Supreme Court Reporter* (discussed later) and some small, rather specialized reporters, the West Publishing Company is the sole publisher of unofficial reporters. They cover all state courts with "Regional Reporters" and all federal courts with three series: *Supreme Court Reporter, Federal Reporter,* and *Federal Supplement.*

These "regionals" are what you would most often use to find reports of cases from the states. West Publishing Company, back in 1880s, decided to systematically and promptly publish all state (and also federal) court decisions. But, instead of publishing an Oregon reporter, a Pennsylvania reporter and so forth, they decided to group all the states into seven regions (plus California and New York which today are separate "regions" of their own). The rationale was that attorneys and courts in any one state would be interested in the deci-

The Pattern of Law Reporting in the United States

State		Federal	
Official	**Unofficial**	**Official**	**Unofficial**
California		**U.S. Supreme Court**	
Supreme Court: *California Reports* ("Cal") Court of Appeals: *California Appellate Reports* ("Cal App")	West Pub. Co.'s *California Reporter* covers all three appellate levels (*viz.*, Supreme Court, Court of Appeals, and the Appellate Departments of the Superior Courts)	*United States Reports*	West Pub. Co.'s *Supreme Court Reporter* Lawyer's Co-Op Pub. Co.'s *United States Supreme Court Reports, Lawyers' Edition* (an annotated reporter)
All States		**U.S. Circuit Courts of Appeal**	
Most states publish their appellate decisions (*e.g., Illinois Reports, Illinois Appellate Court Reports, Oklahoma Reports,* etc.) Some states have adopted the West Pub. Co., reporter as official.	West Pub. Co.'s "Regional Reporters": *Atlantic Reporter:* Conn., Del., D.C., Maine, Md., N.H., N.J., Pa., R.I., and Vt. *North Eastern Reporter:* Ill., Ind., Mass., N.Y., (Court of Appeals only), and Ohio. *North Western Reporter:* Iowa, Mich., Minn., Nebr., N.Dak., S.Dak., and Wis. *Pacific Reporter:* Alaska, Ariz., Calif., (Supreme Court only), Colo., Hawaii, Idaho, Kans., Mont., Nev., N.Mex., Okla., Oreg., Utah, Wash., and Wyo. *South Eastern Reporter:* Ga., N.C., S.C., Va., and W.Va. *Southern Reporter:* Ala., Fla., La., and Miss. *South Western Reporter:* Ark., Ky., Mo., Tenn., and Tex. *New York Supplement:* covers all New York appellate levels. *California Reporter:* covers all California appellate levels.	None	West Pub. Co.'s *Federal Reporter* (also covers miscellaneous other federal courts)
		U.S. District Courts	
		None	West Pub. Co.'s *Federal Supplement* (also covers miscellaneous other federal courts)

sions of surrounding sister states as persuasive authority. In practice this has not happened. For example, the courts of California are far more likely to turn to New York decisions than they are to Nevada decisions for persuasive authority. Despite the mistaken theory, however, the West venture has thrived because their reports generally come out more promptly and with better features (especially the "key number" system—see under digests, *infra*) than the official reports. In several states and the lower federal courts, West provides the only coverage.

5. Parallel Reporters; United States Supreme Court Cases

"Parallel reporters" are reporters that overlap in their coverage. For example, California Supreme Court cases are covered in one official reporter (*California Reports*) and two regional reporters (*California Reporter* and *Pacific Reporter*).

There are also three reporters covering the United States Supreme Court:

a. *United States Reports* is "official." If you looked at this set on the shelves you would see that the early volumes have names on the back (*e.g.*, Cranch, Dallas, Wheton, Peters, *et al.*) These are examples of "nominative reporters" which were named after the editor rather than the jurisdiction covered.
b. *Supreme Court Reporter.* This is a West reporter with the usual features. Looking inside the volumes, you can note the numbers in heavy type inserted, often between sentences, in the text of the opinion. These refer to pages in the official reporter. Take a look at the same case in the official reporter and you will see that West is telling you precisely where a new page starts. This allows you to accurately cite something to the official reporter (which you must do with the Supreme Court of the United States) even though you might not have *United States Reports* in hand. This system is called "star paging," after the early practice of inserting a star at the point where a new page began.
c. *United States Supreme Court Reports, Lawyers' Edition (called "Lawyers' Edition")*. The other major law book publishing company (along with West) is the Lawyers Co-operative/Bancroft-Whitney Publishing Co. They publish an important legal research tool called the *American Law Reports* (ALR). Both ALR and *Lawyers' Edition* provide "annotations" along with the text of the opinions. An annotation is something that follows the report of a case. It is a legal essay dealing with the primary issue of the case. The writer of the annotation will gather all the cases on the subject from all

jurisdictions and analyze and summarize their holdings, making generalizations regarding rules of law (sometimes majority and minority rules) that courts throughout the United States have applied to a particular factual situation.

Take a look in the back of one of the more recent volumes of the *Lawyers' Edition* and you will find that there are annotations for some cases. Note that they also provide star paging within the opinions.

6. Advance Sheets

As with all types of law books, supplementation is very important. Notice that at the end of all of the reporter series on the shelves in a law library, there are paperbound booklets that contain the latest cases. These booklets are called advance sheets. The volume numbers and page numbers are continued from the bound volumes. Actually, the printers use the same plates in printing the bound reports that they used earlier in printing the advance sheets. This allows you to cite cases by actual page number even before they appear in bound volumes.

Many special tables are found in the advance sheets, but as with the bound volumes, the table of cases is all you need be familiar with for now.

In California, the paperbound booklet entitled *California Official Reports; Official Advance Sheets* . . . serves as an advance sheet for both the Supreme Court of California (green sheets) and the California Court of Appeals (white sheets).

7. *U.S. Law Week*

U.S. Law Week might be called a national legal newspaper. It reports from all jurisdictions on decisions, statutes and administrative rulings that the editors consider to be especially significant. Some items are digested and some are reported full text. It comes out in two volumes: "Supreme Court Sections" and "General Law Sections."

It is *the* place in a law library to find the text of the latest decisions of the United States Supreme Court. *U.S. Law Week* is generally received by a library on a Thursday and will contain the text of Supreme Court decisions handed down on that Monday. Complete and current docket records round out the full coverage *Law Week* gives to the Supreme Court.

Outside of the Supreme Court, coverage is selective. But, when you are looking for important recently signed congressional laws, significant state or federal cases, or federal administrative rulings check *Law Week,* for, if it is reported there, you will have it long before you would in the regular sources.

8. Not All Cases Are Reported

Often people inquire at a law library about cases they have heard about, generally in the news media, and are surprised that the library does not have the case. Not all cases are reported.

Generally speaking, only cases that have been appealed and decided on appeal are reported. Do not forget that the purpose for publishing decisions is to record precedents. Only appellate courts make precedents. A trial judge only decides for the litigating parties and is bound by the applicable precedents set by appellate courts above him. He is not bound by the decisions of other trial courts. Despite this rule, however, some trial decisions (with their judicial opinions) are reported (notably federal district court decisions in West's *Federal Supplement*) and do get cited as persuasive but not *binding* authority.

Not all appellate decisions are reported. Some states have decided that too many cases are being reported. Many cases merely decide the controversy between the litigants without adding new precedents to the body of common law. On top of that, the sheer bulk of published decisions hinders the researcher. In California, for instance, Rule 976(b) of the Rules of Court states:

> No opinion of a Court of Appeal or of an appellate department of the superior court shall be published in the Official Reports unless such opinion (1) establishes a new rule of law or alters or modifies an existing rule, (2) involves a legal issue of continuing public interest, or (3) criticizes existing law.

There is a Rule 976(d) that is peculiar to California which declares that Court of Appeal decisions become a nullity the instant the Supreme Court grants a hearing. Therefore, Court of Appeals decisions will sometimes appear in the advance sheets but will be deleted from the bound volume if a hearing has been granted in the meantime. A further California rule (977) prohibits the citing of unpublished opinions.

Many Federal Court of Appeals and District Court cases go unreported. In general, if a case has no precedential value, either an opinion will not be written or if it is written it will not be authorized by the court for publication by West Publishing Co.

For information on unreported cases, often, the only recourse is to write to the clerk of the appropriate court.

Correct Citation Form (cases)

Sevin v. *State Bar,* 8 Cal. 3d 641, 105 Cal. Rptr. 513, 504 P.2d 449 (1973).

The above citation tells you that the *Sevin* case, decided in 1973, can be found in vol. 8, starting on p. 641, of the 3d series of

California Reports; in vol. 105, starting on p. 513, of *California Reporter;* and in vol. 504, starting on p. 449, of the 2d series of *Pacific Reporter.*

There are five parts to a case citation: name, volume, reporter, page and date.

Find the *Sevin* case in all three reporters and notice that the text of the opinion is the same in each. Look also at the title pages of each reporter volume to see how their coverage overlaps on California Supreme Court cases.

B. Shepards (cases)

1. The Purpose of Shepards (cases)

After you have found a case on point, two further questions must be answered before it can be cited as a precedent:

a. *What was the history of the case?* That is, what was the subsequent procedural history, if any? If you have a case from the California Court of Appeals, was it appealed to the Supreme Court of California or of the United States? Did they reverse, affirm or modify? Answers to these questions could dramatically effect the value of your case as precedent.

b. *What was the treatment of the case?* That is, how did subsequent cases which cited your case treat it as precedent? Did they follow it, overrule it, criticize it, or explain it?

The purpose of *Shepard's Citations* for cases is to answer these two preceding questions. If you would look at the first few introductory pages of any volume of Shepard's covering cases you would find some tables labelled "Abbreviations-Analysis." The first two tables of abbreviations dealing with the history and the treatment of a case tell the kinds of information Shepard's can give about a case.

2. How to "Shepardize" a Case

The steps in Shepardizing are as follows:

a. *Find the right Shepards Series.* There is a Shepards for every reporter. They are generally shelved at the end of the reporter series they cover (*e.g., California Shepards* at the end of the various California reporters, *Pacific Shepards* at the end of the *Pacific Reporters,* etc.). Some law libraries will shelve all Shepard's together in one location. Make sure you have the "case edition" and not the "statute edition."

b. *Find all of the supplements.* The general pattern is a basic hard bound compilation with a red paper bound supplement, plus a final uncolored pamphlet supplement.

c. *Find the volume number of the case citation.* On the top of every page in Shepards you will find the name of the reporter covered and the volume number.

d. *Find the page number of the case citation.* The page numbers of case citations are found in heavy type scattered throughout each page of Shepards.

e. *Read and study the list of citations under your case.* Under the page numbers for each case. Shepards gives a list of all the cases, attorney general opinions, the major local and national law reviews, and other sources *that have cited your case.* Abbreviations at the front of some citations tell whether or not the citing case has affirmed, reversed, modified, followed, distinguished, etc., the case. The small superior numbers in the middle of the citations refer to headnote numbers in the case and therefore tell on which point of law it was cited.

f. *Check the tables of abbreviations at the front of Shepards.* No one bothers memorizing the abbreviations Shepards uses for the history and treatment of cases. There are also tables of abbreviations for the titles of the reporters, law reviews, etc., which will need to be referred to because Shepard's uses its own very shortened abbreviations.

g. *Check all the supplements.*

C. Case Finders and Other Tools for Case Law Research

1. Digests

a. How They are Put Together (the Pigeonholes at West's)

A digest is a subject index to cases. It is not the only subject index to cases but it is, by far, the most comprehensive. The components of a digest are fairly simple. If you looked at *West's California Digest* (or *McKinney's,* its competitor) you would find that it is a set of books, about sixty or seventy volumes long. The main body of the set is arranged like an encyclopedia with subjects running from abandonment to zoning. At the beginning there is a multivolumed index called a "Descriptive Word Index." Within each volume of the main set there are page after page of short paragraphs that summarize statements of rules of law from court opinions. Each paragraph concludes with a citation to the case it came from. By my rough calculation there are 600,000 of these little paragraphs arranged under 400 topics. They are subdivided into many thousands of subtopics. (As I recall the first time I looked at a digest, I remember feeling that these were the strangest, driest, most technical and confusing things I had ever seen in print.)

There is no way digests can be made less repulsive; there is, however, a way to remove some of the mystery. Digests are not hard to understand if you know how West goes about putting them together. The following is an only slightly fanciful description of how it is done. (Citations to actual pages and volumes have been included for those few of you who might want to see all of this in the flesh.)

We have to begin with the reports themselves. Everyday at West's, back in St. Paul, Minnesota, written opinions from judges all over the United States are coming across the desks of the "editors." Let us pick out one opinion and follow it through (the case of *People* v. *Smith,* 48 Cal. Rptr. 382). Our editor takes a copy of the opinion, reads it through and then proceeds to encircle *every statement in the opinion that appears to be a statement of a rule of law.* In our case, the editor sees the language at the very beginning of the opinion on page 392 that reads:

> . . . specific intent necessary to commit burglary is simply the felonious design with which the accused enters the building, *i.e.*, "with intent to commit grand or petit larceny or any felony" therein. (Pen. Code, § 459)

He decides that this is a statement by the court of a rule of law and encircles it. Every encircled statement, with a few minor changes in wording for the sake of smooth reading, becomes a "headnote." (See headnote number 13 at the beginning of the report.)

In addition to selecting statements from the opinion as headnotes, our editor also assigns a topic and subtopic heading to each. In this instance he has assigned the heading "Burglary Key no. 3." These headings are selected from West's master classification scheme in which all of American law has been divided into around 400 topics and many thousands of subtopics. Each heading also has a "key number"—merely a shorthand way of identifying these thousands of headings.

Now, we have to imagine that West, for California for instance, has an enormous pigeonhole arrangement with thousands of little pigeonholes, each one labelled with a key number. Then we must picture someone coming along and cutting out each one of the headnotes from all of the current California reports, writing the citation to the case it came from, and then sticking it in its proper hole (along with all the other headnotes from other cases that came under the same key number topic and subtopic).

Our saga continues when another West employee comes along

every few months or so, collects all of these headnotes in their key number order, pastes them onto sheets of paper, has them printed up by a photo offset process and, *voila,* you have the latest supplements to *West's California Digest.* (To prove this to yourself, look in volume 10a of *West's California Digest* under key no. 3, Burglary-Intent, the third paragraph down. You will see that it is word-for-word, the same as headnote number 13 in *People* v. *Smith.*)

So, now you know that a digest is a kind of topical index to statements of rules of law, made in appellate opinions. If you know the difference between holding and dictum (see p. 7), it will be obvious to you that the editors at West make no distinction between the two. There is no attempt made to consider these statements in light of the entire context of the case. Therefore, when you are looking through a digest, trying to find cases which are precedents for certain rules of law (which is what you use a digest for) you cannot be sure you have found a "case on point" merely because the language in the headnote appears to be the very language you are looking for. West is only telling you that such language was used in the case cited and it is up to you to go to the report of the case itself to see, for example, if the rule you are looking for was even at issue in the case. Sometimes West will have twenty or thirty headnotes to one case. No single case, however, could be precedent for so many rules of law.

Let us continue our exciting sojourn through West Country and trace that same old language from the *Smith* case some more. At the end of our last episode we discovered that West had put together its *California Digest* by simply collecting headnotes from the reports and rearranging them according to their classification scheme. West publishes a great many digests. They are published on three different layers: state digests, regional digests; and a single digest that covers the entire United States called the *Decennial Digest.* Generally speaking, the regional digests and the *Decennial Digest* are nothing more than recompilations of all the digests below them. For example, the *Pacific Digest* is simply a rearrangement of the *Alaska Digest, Washington Digest, Oregon Digest, California Digest,* and so forth. In like manner, the *Decennial Digest* incorporates all of the headnotes from all of their state and federal digests. (If you want to verify this, look in the pocket part to volume six of the new series of the *Pacific Digest* under "Key no. 3 Burglary-Intent, Cal. 1966" and in volume five of the *Seventh Decennial Digest.*)

You will notice in tracing this same headnote through different digests, once you find the key number West has assigned to a rule of law in a California or other state case, other cases on that point can be found from any jurisdiction in the United States.

b. Steps in Using a Digest

There are three approaches to using a digest: by case headnotes, by legal concept, or by use of the index.

1. Case headnote approach
   The case headnote approach can be used when you already have one case that is on point and you want to find others. Simply check the headnotes in the West report of the case and find the key numbers you are interested in. Look under these key numbers in the appropriate West digest.
2. Legal concept approach
   The legal concept approach is used when a general area of the law is known quite well. It is the opposite of the index approach.
   a. Select the correct digest (*i.e., California Digest, New York Digest, Federal Practice Digest, United States Supreme Court Digest,* etc.)
   b. Select the volume of the set containing your topic (*e.g.,* Torts in vol. 34 of *West's California Digest*).
   c. Read the "Analysis" on the first page of the topic.
   d. Select the subtopic (*e.g.,* "Torts-Proximate Cause of Injury").
   e. Go to the subtopic and read its detailed analysis.
   f. Select the sub-subtopic (*e.g.,* "Torts-Proximate Cause of Injury-Intervening Efficient Cause").
   g. Look over the digests of cases under the sub-subtopic (or sub-sub-subtopic) and find the case or cases with facts or issues most closely resembling your problem.
   h. Check all supplements.
   i. Note the case citations and look them up to see if they are *really* on point. Merely using "good quotes" from the digest will get you in trouble.
3. Index approach
   Most law students and attorneys use the index approach. The steps are:
   a. Select the correct digest.
   b. Find the several volumes of the "Descriptive Word Index."
   c. Look under all the terms you think would cover your problem. The indexes use practical, everyday words (stepladders, truck drivers, etc.) as well as legal terms.
   d. Note the "key numbers" given in the index.
   e. Look over the digests of cases under the key numbers and find the case or cases with facts or issues most closely resembling your problem.

f. Check all supplements.
g. Note the case citations and look them up to see if they are *really* on point. Merely using "good quotes" from the digest will get you in trouble.

c. *The Decennial Digest*

You will not have much occasion to use this, because as a practical matter, it is very seldom that you will be looking for cases from any or all jurisdictions. Legal research is very specific research: you are trying to convince a judge that he must rule in your favor because in prior situations like yours, the same court or a court superior to it, ruled a certain way.

If the occasion ever arrives, however, when the *Decennial Digest* must be used, it would be helpful to have some notion about its peculiar arrangement. Because of the enormous scope of this digest, West Publishing Co. decided to divide it up into ten year periods. If you were to look at the *Decennial Digest* you would note that it starts out with some volumes labelled "Century Edition, 1658-1896." These are followed by the "Decennial Edition, 1907-1916," and so forth on up through the "Seventh Decennial Digest, 1956-1966." Each one of these "Decennials" (including the "Century Edition") is a separate and complete digest of all state and federal cases for the particular years covered. Each covers all topics from abandonment to zoning. Each is followed by its own table of cases and descriptive word index.

The only thing complicated about the Decennials is looking for cases within the current ten year period (we are now in the 1967-1977 period). This period is being covered by a series of green bound volumes and blue pamphlets called "West's General Digest, Fourth Series." Here, for each year (excluding the current year) there is a separate unit. For example, 1967 is covered in three green hardbound volumes (abandonment to zoning) followed by a table of cases. The descriptive word index is in a separate hardbound blue volume. The most recent headnotes can be found in the blue paper pamphlets. All of these green and blue books and pamphlets will, of course, be replaced by an "Eighth Decennial Digest" in 1978.

d. The Pattern of Publication of Digests

There is a digest for:

Each state (*Alabama Digest*, etc.)

Each West region (*Atlantic Digest*, etc.)

All federal courts (*Modern Federal Practice Digest*). (Note, do not use the *Federal Digest*, it only covers to 1939.)

The United States Supreme Court (West's *United States Supreme Court Digest* and Lawyers Co-op's *U.S. Supreme Court Digest*)
The entire United States (*Decennial Digest*)

2. Secondary Sources as Case Finders

This subject is covered in more detail in the chapter on secondary sources starting on p. 61. It is listed here merely to note that since all legal writing (whether in law reviews, practice texts, legal encyclopedias or elsewhere) is heavily annotated, secondary sources serve as excellent case finders.

3. Words and Phrases

This is also discussed in the chapter on secondary sources. West made use of its case headnotes and put together *Words and Phrases*. Bancroft-Whitney did the same with *California Words and Phrases*. If you are looking for cases that have defined a legal or nonlegal word or phrase, do not forget these sets.

4. Popular Name Tables

There is not much that need be said about these easily understood tools. When the only reference available is the "Flag Salute Cases," a popular names table will need to be used. The most complete listing is *Shepard's Acts and Cases by Popular Names, Federal and State.*

Popular case names are also found in West's *United States Supreme Court Digest* and West's *Decennial Digest.*

5. Parallel Citations: the Blue and White Books; Shepard's

The "Blue" and "White Books" are generally shelved near the West reporters. The Blue Books take you from an official case citation to the West reporter citation. The White Books do the opposite.

Most people find Shepard's case citators are a more convenient source for parallel citations. The first entry under your case will be the parallel citation. It will be enclosed in parentheses.

D. Records and Briefs

When an appeal is filed, the appellant must supply, by statute, a certain number of copies of the record and his brief to the court. The record includes the pleadings filed in the case, relevant parts of the trial testimony, and relevant documentary evidence. The brief is the written argument directed to the appellate court. In addition to going to the judges and opposing counsel, copies of these appellant's and appellee's briefs (and, in some jurisdictions, the records) eventually are sent to certain depository libraries.

The situation from state to state will vary, but we can use California as an example. Most of the large county law libraries and law school libraries in California are depositories for the briefs of the California Supreme Court and the Court of Appeals. The San Francisco and Los Angeles county law libraries are the only official depositories for the records and briefs of the United States Supreme Court; however, all law libraries of any size will have the same in microform. United States Court of Appeals, Ninth Circuit briefs are not widely distributed, but sometimes are available from the State Law Library in Sacramento, the Los Angeles County Law Library, and the University of California law school library at Berkeley.

The briefs can be a great labor saving device in doing legal research. There are no special rewards for doing things the hard way. If you find a case on point why not get the briefs in the case and have the benefit of somebody else's work product. In cities, where there are large libraries that have records and briefs, they are a favorite research tool.

CHAPTER V

TREATIES

There is a tendency to regard treaty research as the very specialized concern of international lawyers, but there are a number of everyday occurrences which are governed by provisions of treaties to which the United States is a part.* For example, when an American citizen earns income in a foreign country that has an income tax, he has a potential problem of double taxation which may be provided for in a treaty between the two countries. Another common situation covered by bilateral treaties is that of the distribution of property located in another country but owned by an American decedent. Treaties, of course, are of central importance in the entire area of international business transactions, including such matters as tariffs, trade, copyright, patent, and trademark. Finally, conservation (particularly of marine resources) is often a matter for treaty coverage.

There are many different sets of books an expert might use in doing treaty research but for the purposes of this manual, only three will be covered:

a. For the text of United States treaties before 1950: *Statutes at Large*
b. For the text of United States treaties since 1950: *United States Treaties and Other International Agreements*
c. For an index of United States treaties currently in force: *Treaties in Force*

The officially published text of U.S. Treaties until 1950 was found in a part of *Statutes at Large.* In 1950 the federal government started a new series: *United States Treaties and Other International Agreements.*

There is no really good index to all of the current treaty provisions. All we have is an annual publication called *Treaties in Force.* As the title indicates, it only covers treaties currently in force. If you looked at

*Art. 6, clause 2 of the United States Constitution provides that treaties, along with the Constitution and the enactments of Congress, are "the supreme law of the land."

a copy of *Treaties in Force,* you would see that it merely is a listing of treaties to which the United States is a party. It is divided into two parts: bilateral treaties and multilateral treaties. The bilateral treaties are listed by country and the multilateral treaties are listed by subject.

CHAPTER VI

SECONDARY SOURCES

A. Introduction

If you wanted to find out under what circumstances if any, photocopying in a library of copyrighted materials is an infringement, you could start your research with several different sources. If you knew that copyright is a federal matter under the Constitution, you might go to title 17 ("Copyrights") of the United States Code to see what laws Congress has passed on the subject. Your search would prove fruitless, however, because at the time of this writing the original 1909 law stands virtually unamended and, of course, does not anticipate the current extensive use of photocopy machines. Since you would find no statutory law on the subject, you might then turn to case law to see what the courts may have said. The basic tool for locating cases on a subject is called a digest. After a great deal of searching through the digest for federal cases you would have found, with luck, the *one decided case* on library photocopying. You might then ask yourself, "Is this all there is?" With the thousands of libraries in the United States that have photocopy machines (many of which have signs that caution the user about the possibility of infringement), you might expect to find more information on the subject than just one case. The answer is that a law library will have a lot of "information" on the subject, it is just that there is very little *law* on the subject. For example, there are many law review articles, several books, and government documents on this topic.

The point is that the researcher would have made a mistake on two counts by starting his research with primary materials. First of all, he would have floundered around a great deal in the indexes because he *did not know the subject.* Actually, library photocopying comes under copyright within the "fair use" doctrine. Without knowing this, a lot of time would have been lost. Secondly, as with many current legal topics, there has not been much law (statutes, cases, administrative regulations, etc.) developed.

It cannot be stressed too strongly that inexperienced and busy legal researchers should make themselves familiar with the many secondary sources in literature. They are invaluable for a quick overview and introduction to a topic. In addition, they all have copious annotations to primary sources and, thus, will also serve as search books to statutes, cases, administrative regulations, and other sources of law.

B. *American Law Reports* (*ALR*)

ALR is an annotated reporter with indexes and supplements. It is currently in a third series. The accompanying chart illustrates this.

1. What is an "Annotated Reporter"?

ALR selects cases from throughout the country that are particularly good illustrations of points of law (because of the facts, the opinion, or both). Since it reports the opinions of these cases, it is a reporter.

An annotation follows each opinion. The annotation is a legal essay on the point of law illustrated by the selected case. It will give the issues involved in this point of law and will summarize the various rules (majority and minority rules) which hold in all jurisdictions that have decisions on point. The annotation will also give citations to all cases and arrange them by jurisdiction. In many situations research can begin and end here. Among the thousands of annotations in the various series of *ALR* there is a good chance you will find one on your point of law.

ALR: An Annotated Reporter with Indexes and Supplements

Series	Annotated Reports	Indexes			Supplements
1st	*ALR* (175 vol.)	*Permanent ALR Digest* (12 vol.)	*ALR Word Index* (4 vol.)	*ALR 1st Series Quick Index* (1 vol.)	*ALR Blue Book of Supplemental Decisions* (4 vol. and paper supplement)
2nd	*ALR2d* (100 vol.)	ALR2d *Digest* (7 vol.)	*ALR Word Index* (3 vol.)	*ALR Quick Index, Second Edition* (1 vol.)	*ALR2d Later Case Service* (15 vol. and pocket parts)
3rd	*ALR3d* (66 vol. to date)			*ALR Quick Index, Second Edition* (1 vol. + pocket part)	pocket parts in each volume.
Federal	*ALR Federal* (25 vol. to date)			*Federal Quick Index*	pocket parts in each volume.

2. Indexes and Supplements

If you understand what these annotations are and what you can use them for, you should ask yourself what else would such a valuable research tool need. It would need two things: indexes and supplements. This is what all the rest of those red, blue, and other colored books on the shelves are. All of them are either providing a way to find the annotation you want or updating an annotation you have already found.

Why are there so many of these indexes and supplements and why do they have so many different names? One thing you can do to bring some order to all this is to realize that each series (*ALR, ALR2d, ALR3d* and *ALR Federal*) has its own set of indexes and supplements. Unfortunately, the names, colors, and form of these indexes and supplements have changed somewhat over the fifty some years the publishers have been putting out *ALR*.

Take a look at the accompanying chart and we will talk about indexes and supplements.

a. Indexes

Notice in the chart that *ALR* and *ALR2d* have three different indexes. In the earlier days of this publication the editors wanted to give two different ways of finding an annotation: a digest approach and a word approach. Later on they came out with a third index that combined both approaches.

The digests were an hierarchical arrangement of headnotes (the same things you see in the West digests) under major headings followed by successively narrower subheadings. To use this tool, an analytical approach must be used. For example, you would have to know that calling a thief a thief is called pleading the truth and that is a defense to an action called slander which comes under the general area of intentional torts. I do not know of anyone who ever uses the digest or analytical approach to *ALR*—so, forget about the *Permanent ALR Digest* and the *ALR2d Digest*.

Next, there are the *ALR Word Index* and *ALR2d Word Index*. They are like other indexes you have used. You must look under specific factual or legal terms to find a reference to your annotation.

The third type of index which can be found is fairly new; it is the "quick index." The quick index attempts two things: first, it includes both specific type index entries (like in the word indexes) and analytical type entries (like in the digests); secondly, it does it all in one volume. It is like a Detroit compact: smaller on the outside but bigger on the inside. In actual fact, **the quickest index is the biggest index.** Nothing wastes your time more than being unable to find what you want because the indexer has only listed it under one term instead of the five or six different terms a person might reasonably expect to find it under. In summary, to find an annotation in *ALR* or *ALR2d* use the four volume *Word Index* for *ALR* and the three volume *Word Index* for *ALR2d.* For *ALR3d* there is only a "quick index."

b. Supplements

After one of the indexes has led you to the desired annotation, you will need to update it. This means two things: first, you will want citations to later cases on the same point and secondly, you will want to find out if yours is the latest annotation. Over the years, as the law changes, the editors will write new annotations that completely supersede older annotations. As you can imagine, many of the annotations in *ALR* have been replaced in *ALR2d* or *3d.* On the chart you can see that *ALR* has its "Blue Book," *ALR2d* has its "Later Case Service," and *ALR3d* and *ALR Federal* do what they should have done all along . . . provide pocket parts, just as supplementation is done in other law books.

Correct Citation Form

Annot., 1 *ALR3d* 677 (1965)

C. Encyclopedias

These are easy to use. They all have multi-volumed indexes. The only questions are: When do you use them? How good are they?

You should be familiar with the two national encyclopedias: *American Jurisprudence* (*Am Jur*) and *Corpus Juris Secundum* (*CJS*). In California there is *California Jurisprudence* (*Cal Jur*). Many other states also have an encyclopedia.

A legal encyclopedia synthesizes and arranges the case law within its jurisdictional coverage. If you picked up a volume of *Am Jur* you would see that it is an arrangement of "black-letter" (pithy summaries) statements of law with copious case citations. Legal encyclopedias have two drawbacks. One, they do not cover statutes to any significant extent. Two, they often overgeneralize and do not reflect the complexity of changing law. For example, *Cal Jur* would be a poor place to go for a search and seizure problem. However, they often can be valuable as a quick overview in an unfamiliar area of the law and, because of the plentiful citations, as a case finder.

Correct Citation Form

17 *CJS* Contracts § 16, at 615 (1963)

17 *Am Jur* 2d Contracts § 171 (1964)

12 *Cal Jur* 2d Contracts § 22 (1953)

D. Words and Phrases

If you looked inside West Publishing Co.'s *Words and Phrases*, you would see that they made even further use of their case headnotes (see Digests, p. 49). They have simply taken all those headnotes that dealt with definitions (legal *and* nonlegal) and arranged them under the words and phrases being defined. It can be a very useful and often overlooked case finder when the issue being researched is a question of definition.

Bancroft-Whitney publishes *California Words, Phrases and Maxims*.

E. Periodicals (Law Reviews)

1. Their Purpose

Why do we have law reviews? Part of the answer is "publish or perish" in the law faculties and part of the answer is that law reviews, like other scholarly periodicals, fill the need for literature on topics that are *very current* or *very specific*. Most of us know this intuitively, but often when a problem comes up that calls for looking up an article on the subject, we do not think in terms of periodicals. For example, if our topic were legalized abortion, the best place to begin would be the *Index to Legal Periodicals*. The topic is too current for any large body of case law to have developed on it. Also it is probably too narrow and too dynamic for a reliable and complete treatise on the subject.

2. Their Use (*The Index to Legal Periodicals*)

Another advantage of periodicals is that the contents are so accessible. Most people find the *Index to Legal Periodicals* one of the easier sets to use in a law library. Articles are indexed by author and subject. The indexes are quite current and are published monthly. Most people have used periodical indexes as undergraduates, particularly the *Reader's Guide to Periodical Literature*. The *Index to Legal Periodicals* is published by the same company and arranged essentially the same way. It is usually best to start your search with a list of subject headings which can be found at the beginning of any of the volumes. The list is not especially long and time will be saved by going through it and making a list of all the possible headings under which you might find your topic. This way you are less likely to overlook a heading that the editors might have used for your topic.

The *Index to Legal Periodicals* is presently divided into "Subject and Author Index," "Table of Cases Commented Upon," and "Book Review Index." In the subject/author index, full entries are only given under the subject. Looking under author, you would get a reference like "Legal history (C)" which means it would be necessary to look under the subject "Legal history" and them to look for an article with a title that starts with the letter "C."

3. Other Periodical Indexes

People from other disciplines besides law are interested in many legal topics. This literature can be found through such other periodical indexes as *Business Periodicals Index, Social Sciences and Humanities Index, Applied Science and Technology Index,* and the *Public Affairs Information Service.*

Correct Citation Form (articles in legal periodicals)

Ayer, *Water Quality Control at Lake Tahoe,* 58 Calif. L. Rev. 1273 (1970)

F. Practice Texts and Treatises

1. General Finding Tools

Practice texts and treatises is a broad category covering a number of different kinds of books on legal subjects. The main difficulty with using these books is that people often forget about them when doing research. It is foolish for a busy practitioner or other researcher to assemble all of the cases, statutes, regulations, etc., on an area of the law and then attempt to put them all together into some coherent legal argument, if someone else has written a reliable book on the same subject.

The primary tool for finding out if a library has a book on a certain subject is the card catalog. Another good source is advice from subject specialists. Many titles will be found through the use of footnotes and other references you may encounter in using other law books. Librarians can often tell you what titles are most often used. At appendix B there is a subject list of popular texts.

2. Hornbooks

These are one volume student texts. They provide a summary treatment of law school subjects. (Example, *Prosser on Torts.*)

3. Practice Books

These are designed especially for the practicing lawyer. They often have a "how to do it" style. California and the attorneys of some other states are especially fortunate because of the great number of texts on state law put out by the state's "Continuing Education of the Bar." On a national scale, the American Law Institute-American Bar Association handbooks and those of the Practicing Law Institute are often excellent introductions to unfamiliar areas of the law.

4. Standard Treatises

There are a number of definitive respected treatises on major legal topics. They are generally large multi-volume sets that are well supplemented and have been in publication for a number of years. Examples include: *Wigmore* for evidence, *Davis*, for administrative law, *Couch* for insurance, and *Sutherland* for statutory construction. The standard treatises have been cited many times by the courts. Glance over the case of *Executive Jet Aviation, Inc.* v. *City of Cleveland*, 409 U.S. 249 (1973) and see how much the Supreme Court of the United States cites *Benedict on Admiralty* and *Moore on Federal Practice.*

5. Witkin's Publications

B. E. Witkin of the San Francisco Bar is a remarkable man with appetite large enough to feed on all of the California law. He is California's Blackstone.

Witkin's publications—*Summary of California Law, Evidence, California Procedure, Crimes,* and *Criminal Procedure*—comprise a complete encyclopedia of California case and statute law. Unlike the state encyclopedias, "Witkin" is not the mechanical production of an anonymous team. In these works, one intellect has digested California law and produced a summary which is "practical, concise, selective and critical." He has done much of the weeding and weighing you would have to do yourself. His works have been very popular with the California bar for a great many years.

Correct Citation Form (practice texts and treatises)
W. Prosser, *Handbook of the Law of Torts* § 96 (4th ed. 1971)

G. Looseleaf Services

At a minimum, you have now learned that legal research is time consuming and the bibliography is complex. This is obviously a critical problem for a practicing lawyer. There are few clients willing to fund, at a rate of fifty dollars or so an hour, extensive sojourns through the labyrinth of a law library.

The documentation in some areas of the law is especially complex. Federal income tax law, for example, is found in Congress's Internal Revenue Code, the Treasury Department's Regulations, the Internal Revenue Service's rulings, the U.S. Tax Court's decisions, and the U.S.

Court of Appeal's decisions. These are all separate sets of books with their own peculiar arrangement, indexing, and method of supplementing. Since most of these sets are government publications, the indexing is mostly inadequate or nonexistent and the supplementing is generally not prompt. On top of that, these are only the primary sources for the text of the law; one would still have to search elsewhere for expert commentary, explanation, or summary.

The solution offered to this problem by the law book publisher is the "looseleaf service." Attorneys who subscribe to these services seldom have to research beyond the service. A looseleaf service is generally a multivolumed set in three ring or post binders that:

1. Compiles the text of all the laws (cases, statutes, regulations, etc.) on one topic.
2. Provides editorial comment (*i.e.,* serves as a textbook).
3. Provides a subject index to the entire topic.
4. Provides "finding lists" (*i.e.,* enables you to get into the text of the law or the commentary via a citation to a case, statute, regulation etc.).
5. Provides information on new and pending developments on the topic (often in the form of a weekly newsletter).
6. Provides other special features, *e.g.,*
   a. case citators
   b. forms
   c. calendars
   d. glossaries
   e. checklists
7. Provides very frequent supplementation by means of individual "replacement pages." (Often, a subscriber will receive a package of new pages weekly which will completely replace various pages scattered throughout the service.)

Looseleaf services that provide reports of cases really serve as a typical reporter. Recent cases will appear in the looseleaf binders as "advance sheets" which, at the end of the year, will cummulate into bound volumes. For example, the Commerce Clearing House, Inc., *Standard Federal Tax Reporter* is accompanied by over one hundred hardbound volumes of *U.S. Tax Cases* and over thirty volumes of *Tax Court Memorandum Decisions.* The text of administrative regulations will also sometimes accompany the service in a series of volumes.

Because of the variety of features and arrangements found among the various looseleaf services, it is not feasible to provide a step-by-step explanation of how to use them. **But, there is an index.** If you will regard a looseleaf service as a multi-volumed treatise that also contains the full text of the law and locate the index (often called "topical index")—you will be able to use it for most purposes. Moreover, each service will contain detailed instructions for use at the beginning of the set.

Looseleaf services are available on many legal topics, especially in those areas that are dynamic and complex. This is particularly true of activities that are extensively regulated by administrative agencies.

H. Form Books

1. General

A great deal of legal practice includes the drafting or filling out of the right piece of paper. There are contracts, pleadings, wills, deeds, leases, applications and so forth. As soon as you are faced with the necessity for one of these pieces of paper, you will want to see how others have done it before. You will want to see samples. A law firm will keep a file of the forms it has used for later reference, but the largest number of sample forms are found in published "form books."

These are not necessarily the product of experts who have sat down and drafted perfect forms. Rather, they are collections of forms that have actually been used. The publishers, for the most part, get them from court records and from the files of law offices that wish to get their names in print. These forms cannot be used verbatim because there never could be a collection large enough to cover all situations. Also, there is no guarantee that they are the best—only that they have been used before.

2. Types of Form Books

The only difficulty in using form book sets is in knowing which type to use. There are two main types of form book sets and several other special sources of forms:

a. *Business (or Substantive) Form Books.* This is the most general type of form book. It will include many kinds of contracts, estate planning forms, commercial transactions, and real estate transactions—just about everything except forms you would send to a court (pleadings, etc.). The most popular set for California is probably Matthew Bender's *California Legal Forms: Transaction Guide.* Other form books are published for the larger states. *Am Jur Legal Forms* is a good business form book that is not tied to any particular jurisdiction.
b. *Procedural Form Books.* This is the other major type of form book. These often go under the title of pleading and practice forms. Here you will find forms that are directed to a court.

Matthew Bender's *California Forms of Pleading and Practice: Annotated* is popular. Other states will have their own.

c. *Code Form Books.* These are form books that accompany an annotated code. They will use the same title and section numbers as the codes. Any time a code section requires the use of a form you can check the accompanying code form book. In California, West publishes its *California Code Forms* to accompany its annotated code. Deering's has code forms also, but they are set out in the annotated codes themselves. Many other states will have the same.

d. *Special Form Books.* Some form books are designed for a single type of activity. Examples of these are Matthew Bender's *California Points and Authorities* and Bender's *Forms of Discovery.*

e. *Textbooks and Treatises.* Many textbooks and treatises, especially those oriented toward the general practitioner, will have forms.

APPENDIX A

RESEARCH STRATEGY CHARTS

RESEARCH STRATEGY CHART 1

Steps to Take When You Are Reasonably Familiar with the Area of the Law

I. *Check the Statutes First!*
   A. For California, go to *West's* or *Deering's* (or similar state annotated code).
   B. For federal, go to *USCA*.
   C. The steps are: general index to bound volume to pocket part to pamphlet supplement and advanced legislative service.
   D. The annotations will lead you to cases.
      1. Shepardize the cases.
   E. Legislative history?
      1. Use *CCH Congressional Index* or *U.S. Code: Congressional and Administrative News*.
      2. See Documents Librarian.

II. *When There Is No Statute: Use a Digest to Find Cases.*
   A. For California, go to *West's* or *McKinney's* (or similar state digest).
   B. For federal, go to the *Modern Federal Practice Digest*.
   C. "Descriptive Word Index" uses legal and nonlegal terms. Think of the kinds of people involved, the place where the action occurred, the instrumentality involved, the cause of action or defense, and the relief sought.
   D. Check the supplement.
   E. Shepardize.

III. *Are There Administrative Regulations?*
   A. For California go to the *California Administrative Code* (or similar state administrative code, if available).
      1. There is no index—use the "Table of Titles" at the beginning of volume 1.
      2. It is kept current with weekly replacement pages (looseleaf format).
      3. The *California Blue Book* (or similar state manual) will tell you how the state government is organized.

B. For federal go to *CFR*.
   1. Use the "Index" volume and its supplements.
   2. Update what you find in *CFR*.
      a. Tables of "Code Sections Affected" will lead you to the *Federal Register* (comes out daily).
   3. The *United States Government Manual* will tell how the federal government is organized.

RESEARCH STRATEGY CHART 2

Where to Go When You Do Not Know Where to Start

I. Use the *Index to Legal Periodicals* when:
There is not much law on the topic, the topic is very recent, the topic is popular, you are looking for policy arguments, or the topic is too narrow for a textbook.
   A. Check the list of subject headings in the front before going into the body of the index.
   B. If the topic is nonlegal or quasi-legal check the other periodical indexes.

II. Use *ALR* when:
There are few or no cases from your state and you want persuasive authority from other states, you do not have much time, or you want to see both sides of the question.
   A. Use the "Word Indexes" for *ALR* and *ALR2d* and the "Quick Index" for *ALR3d.*
   B. Check the supplements for each series for later cases and superseding annotations.

III. Use *Practice Texts* or *Treatises* when they exist.
   A. To find out if there is a book on your subject, look in the card catalog, ask a subject specialist, or ask a librarian.
   B. Standard treatises are good persuasive authority.
   C. Don't forget the Continuing Education of the Bar books.

IV. Use the *Encyclopedias* when there are no texts or treatises.
   A. *Witkin* is always a good place to start for California questions.
   B. *Cal Jur* is the California encyclopedia. Most other states have similar encyclopedias.
   C. *Am Jur* and *CJS* are the national encyclopedias.

RESEARCH STRATEGY CHART 3

Special Problems

I. *Attorney Generals' Opinions*
   A. They are good persuasive authority.

II. *Form Books*
   A. California court forms: Matthew Bender's *California Forms of Pleading and Practice.* (Similar for most other states.)
   B. California business forms: Matthew Bender's *California Legal Forms.* (Similar for most other states.)
   C. General United States forms: the various *Am Jur* form books.
   D. Federal court forms: Wright and Miller, *Federal Practice and Procedure.*

III. *Local Law*
   A. City and county codes are sometimes available. Otherwise, inquire at the seat of government.

IV. *Legal Directories*
   A. All legal directories are arranged by city. You must know the city in which he or she practices.
   B. California: *California Legal Directory.*
   C. United States: *Martindale-Hubbell.*
      1. Also, the "Law Digests" are excellent summaries of state and foreign statute law.

V. *Parallel Citations?*
   A. Shepard's (parallel citations are given in parenthesis).
   B. Blue and White books.

VI. *Partial Citation?*
   A. When you only have the names of the parties, go to the "Table of Cases" in the appropriate digest to get the full citation.

VII. *Popular Name?*
   A. Use *Shepard's Acts and Cases by Popular Names.*
   B. Some digests and annotated statutes also have popular name tables.

VIII. *Records and Briefs*
   A. When you have a case on point, get the brief too. Pick somebody else's brain.
IX. *Restatements*
   A. They are excellent persuasive authority for statements of "black letter law."
   B. Use *Restatement in the Courts* and the advance sheets of *Shepard's* for cases citing the restatements.
X. *Treaties*
   A. Texts of United States treaties:
      1. Prior to 1950—*Statutes at Large.*
      2. Post 1950—*U.S. Treaties. . . .*
   B. Indexed in:
      1. *Treaties in Force.*
XI. *Uniform Laws*
   A. Found in *Uniform Laws Annotated* (*ULA*).
XII. *Words and Phrases*
   A. A good case finder when the issue is the definition of a word or phrase.

APPENDIX B

A SUBJECT LIST OF TEXTS FREQUENTLY USED BY PRACTICING LAWYERS

(Including Texts of National Scope and California Texts)

Accounting

Finney and Miller. Principles of Accounting: Introduction.
Rappaport. SEC Accounting Practice and Procedure.
CEB. The Lawyer's Use of Financial Statements.

Administrative Law

Cooper. State Administrative Law.
Davis. Administrative Law Treatise.
CEB. California Administrative Agency Practice.
CEB. California Administrative Mandamus.

Admiralty

Benedict. Admiralty.
Knauth. American Law of Ocean Bills of Lading.
Norris. The Law of Seamen.

Agency and Partnership

ALI. Restatement of the Law, Second, Agency.
Bromberg. Crane and Bromberg on Partnership.
Mechem. Outlines of the Law of Agency.
Seavey. Handbook of the Law of Agency.

Antitrust and Trade Regulation

BNA. Antitrust and Trade Regulation Report.
Callmann. Unfair Competition, Trademarks and Monopolies.
CCH. Trade Regulation Reporter.
CEB. Private Federal Antitrust Actions.

Arbitration

Domke. The Law and Practice of Commercial Arbitration.

Automobile

Blashfield. Automobile Law and Practice.
Magana. Motor Vehicle Accidents (Calif.).

Aviation

Billyou. Air Law.
CCH. Aviation Law Reports.
Kreindler. Aviation Accident Law.

Banks and Banking

CCH. Federal Banking Law Reporter.

Commercial Law

Anderson. Uniform Commercial Code.

Bender's Uniform Commercial Code Service.
Callaghan and Co. Uniform Commercial Code Reporting Service.
CCH. Consumer Credit Guide and Secured Transactions Guide.
Gilmore. Security Interests in Personal Property.
CEB. California Commercial Law.
CEB. California Retail Installment Sales.
CEB. Drafting Agreements for the Sale of Business.
CEB. Truth in Lending.

Community Property

DeFuniak. Principles of Community Property.

Conflict of Laws

ALI. Restatement of the Law of Conflict of Laws.
Ehrenzweig. Treatise on the Conflict of Laws.
Leflar. American Conflicts Law.

Constitutional Law

Antieau. Modern Constitutional Law.
U.S. Government Printing Office. The Constitution of the United States of America Annotated.

Contracts

ALI. Restatement of the Law of Contracts.
CCH. Government Contracts Reports.
Corbin. Corbin on Contracts.
Williston. Treatise on the Law of Contracts.

Copyright

Lindey. Entertainment, Publishing and the Arts.
Nimmer. Nimmer on Copyright.

Corporations and Partnerships

CCH. Corporation Law Guide.
Fletcher. Cyclopedia of the Law of Private Corporations.
Matthew Bender. Business Organizations.
O'Neal. Close Corporations.
Ballantine and Sterling. California Corporation Laws.
CEB. Advising California Partnerships.
CEB. Attorney's Guide to California Professional Corporations.
CEB. California Nonprofit Corporations.
CEB. Organizing Corporations in California.

Criminal Law and Procedure

Anderson. Wharton's Criminal Law and Procedure.
BNA. Criminal Law Reporter.

Orfield. Criminal Procedure Under the Federal Rules.
Perkins. Criminal Law.
Torcia. Wharton's Criminal Evidence.
Bell's Searches, Seizures and Bugging Compendium.
California Jury Instructions: Criminal; CALJIC (West Pub. Co.).
California Jury Instructions: Misdemeanor, CALJIC (West Publ. Co.)
CEB. California Juvenile Court Practice.
CEB. California Search and Seizure Practice.
Witkin. California Crimes.
Witkin. California Criminal Procedure.

Debtor and Creditor

Collier. Collier on Bankruptcy.
CCH. Bankruptcy Law Reports.
CCH. Consumer Credit Guide.
CCH. Secured Transactions Guide.
Remington. Treatise on the Bankruptcy Law of the United States.
CEB. California Debt Collection Practice.
CEB. California Mechanics' Liens and Other Remedies.
CEB. Debt Collection Tort Practice.
CEB. Personal Bankruptcies and Wage Earner Plans.
Marsh. California Mechanics' Lien Law Handbook.

Domestic Relations

Lindey. Separation Agreements and Ante-Nuptial Contracts.
Nelson. Divorce and Annulment with Selected Forms.
CEB. California Marital Termination Settlements.
CEB. Family Law Act Practice.

Environment

BNA. Environment Reporter.
Environmental Law Institute. Environmental Law Reporter.

Equity

Pomeroy. A Treatise on Equity Jurisprudence as Administered in the United States of America.

Estates and Estate Planning

Bogert. Trusts and Trustees.
Casner. Estate Planning.
Page on the Laws of Wills.
Prentice Hall. Estate Planning.
Scott. The Law of Trusts.
Simes and Smith. The Law of Future Interests.

CEB. California Conservatorships.
CEB. California Decedent Estate Administration.
CEB. California Probate Workflow Manual.
CEB. California Will Drafting.
CEB. California Will Forms Manual.
CEB. Drafting California Irrevocable Intervivos Trusts.
CEB. Drafting California Revocable Intervivos Trusts.
CEB. Managing an Estate Planning Practice.
Marshall. California Procedure.

Evidence

Wigmore. Evidence.
CEB. California Evidence Benchbook.
CEB. Trial Attorney's Evidence Code Notebook.
Witkin. California Evidence.

Food, Drugs, and Cosmetics

CCH. Food, Drug, Cosmetic Law Reporter.
Toulmin. The Law of Foods, Drugs, Cosmetics.

Government Contracts

CCH. Government Contracts Reporter.
McBride and Wachtel. Government Contracts: Cyclopedic Guide to Law, Administration, and Procedure.

Insurance

Appleman. Insurance Law and Practice.
CCH. Automobile Insurance Law Reports.
CCH. Fire and Casualty Insurance Law Reports.
CCH. Life-Health and Accident Insurance Law Reports.
CCH. Negligence Insurance Law Reports.
Couch. Cyclopedia of Insurance.
Long. The Law of Liability Insurance.
CEB. California Automobile Insurance Law Guide.

Labor

BNA. Labor Relations Reporter.
CCH. Labor Law Reporter.

Mining

Rocky Mountain Mineral Law Foundation. American Law of Mining.

Municipal Corporations

Antieau. Municipal Corporation Law.
McQuillin. Law of Municipal Corporations.

Patents

Deller. Deller's Walker on Patents.

Practice and Procedure (including forms)—Federal

Cyclopedia of Federal Procedure.
Moore's Federal Practice.
Stern and Gressman. Supreme Court Practice.
Wright and Miller. Federal Practice and Procedure.

Practice and Procedure (including forms)—California

Bancroft-Whitney. California Practice, with forms.
California Jury Instructions: Civil; BAJI (West Pub. Co.).
CEB. Attorney's Guide to California Jurisdiction and Process.
CEB. California Attorney's Damages Guide.
CEB. California Civil Appellate Practice.
CEB. California Civil Writs.
CEB. California Trial Objections.
CEB. Essentials of Cross Examination.
Louisell and Wally. Modern California Discovery.
Matthew Bender. California Forms of Pleading and Practice.
Matthew Bender. California Legal Forms; Transaction Guide.
Matthew Bender. California Points and Authorities.
West. California Practice.
Witkin. California Procedure.

Practice and Procedure (including forms)—General

Am Jur Legal Forms.
Am Jur Pleading and Practice Forms.
Am Jur Proof of Facts.
Am Jur Trials.
Bender's Forms of Discovery.
Bender's Forms of Interrogatories.
Nichols Cyclopedia of Legal Forms.
Schweitzer. Cyclopedia of Trial Practice.
West. Modern Legal Forms.

Property

Casner. American Law of Property.
Powell. Law of Real Property.
Thompson. Commentaries on the Modern Law of Real Property.
CEB. California Eviction Defense Manual.
CEB. California Real Estate Sale Transactions.
CEB. California Real Estate Syndicates.
CEB. California Zoning Practice.

CEB. Condemnation Practice in California.
CEB. Ground Lease Practice.
CEB. Guide to California Subdivision Sales Law.
CEB. Ogden's Revised California Real Property Law.
CEB. Secured Real Estate Transactions.
Miller and Starr. Current Law of California Real Estate.

Restitution

ALI. Restatement of Restitution.

Securities

CCH. Blue Sky Law Reporter.
CCH. Federal Securities Law Reporter.
Loss. Securities Regulation.
Prentice Hall. Securities Regulation.
CEB. California Stock Qualification and Exemption.
Marsh and Volk. Practice Under the California Corporate Securities Laws.

Social Legislation

CCH. Poverty Law Reporter.
CCH. Urban Affairs Reporter.

Statutory Construction

Sutherland. Statutes and Statutory Construction.

Taxation

Bureau of National Affairs. Tax Management.
CCH. Inheritance, Estate, and Gift Tax Reports.
CCH. Standard Federal Tax Reports.
Mertens. Law of Federal Income Taxation.
Prentice Hall. Federal Taxes.
Rabkin and Johnson. Federal Income, Gift, and Estate Taxation.
Research Institute of America, Inc., Federal Tax Coordinator.
Ehrman. Taxing California Property.
Rice. California Family Tax Planning.
CEB. California Inheritance Tax Practice.

Torts

ALI. Restatement of the Law, Second, Torts.
Averbach. Handling Accident Cases.
CCH. Products Liability Reporter.
Frumer and Friedman. Products Liability.
Harper and James. Law of Torts.

Larson. The Law of Workmen's Compensation.
Louisell and Williams. Medical Malpractice.
Matthew Bender. Courtroom Medicine.
Matthew Bender. Personal Injury (series).
Prosser. Handbook of the Law of Torts.
CEB. California Government Tort Liability and Supplement.
CEB. California Personal Injury Proof.
CEB. California Tort Guide.
CEB. California Uninsured Motorist Practice.
CEB. California Workmen's Compensation Practice.
Cotchett and Cartwright. California Products Liability Actions.

Water

Water and Water Rights. (Allen Smith Co. Pub.)
Hutchins. California Law of Water Rights.
Rogers and Nichols. Water for California.

Zoning

Anderson. American Law of Zoning.
Rathkopf. The Law of Zoning and Planning.
Yokley. Zoning Law and Practices.
CEB. California Zoning Practice.

Index